REPAIRING THE BREACH

Peter Gunnar Rambo, Sr.

DEDICATION

I dedicate this book to my father,

Gunnar Lloyd Rambo, Jr.

He always challenged and encouraged me, but entered his rest before I began ministry and this journey. This book encompasses a conversation I was never able to have with him, though I firmly believe he would have relished the discussion and would have quickly grasped the truths contained herein. His love of truth and desire to pursue it at all costs rests firmly at the core of my being.

Thank you daddy, and I look forward to exploring this with you in the Kingdom! Shalom!

Peter G. Rambo, Sr.

CONTENTS

Acknowledgments		vii
Foreword		ix
1	Restoration!	1
2	Reformation	5
	RT: Names	6
	RT: Olam!	10
	RT: Grafting	14
	RT: Manipulatives	19
	RT: Anti-Semitism	23
	RT: Riches	32
	RT: Syncretism	36
	RT: Signs	41
	RT: Righteousness	47
	RT: Torah	52
3	Considering the Sabbath	55
	Christians, please help me understand...	56
	Can God 'unsanctify' the 'sanctified?'	61
	"all flesh" ... (Does that include errant theologians?)	64
	'first day of the week,' – Acts 20:7	66
	Countermanding the Almighty	73
4	Paradigm Shifter	81
	10 Paradigm-shifting New Testament verses	83
	10 Paradigm-shifting Old Testament verses	91

5   What About Jesus?   101

      Was Jesus on Mt. Sinai? Does it matter?   102

      Was Jesus on Mt. Sinai? Pt. 2   106

      What did Moses see in the 'burning bush?'   108

      Angel of the Lord Study Guide   113

6   Doctrines of Men   116

      The Error of Dividing the Law   117

      Of elephants and theologians...   125

      Westminster Confession Errors, Pt.1   130

7   It is all about the Kingdom   139

      Yeshua on the Kingdom of Israel   141

      Excellent Passage Defending Messianic Torah   145
      Observance

8   But, but, but,...What about Paul?   147

      The Apostle Paul was NOT a Christian   149

      What was Paul's Example?   153

9   Repairing the Breach   157

      Dividing of Israel and Judah, Then and Now   158

      The Sin of Israel and Modern Christianity   163

   Resources   170

   About the Author   171

   Scripture Index   173

Peter G. Rambo, Sr.

ACKNOWLEDGMENTS

First, and towering over all others, is YHVH, the God of Abraham, Isaac and Jacob, the Everlasting and Unchanging Self-Existing One who called me from darkness and caused me to crossover and be His child with an inheritance and a destiny. It is His gracious plan and purpose being worked out in the world and among His Chosen People that so excites me.

In addition to my Heavenly Father's leading and influence, there are many, many others who have encouraged or in some way pushed me forward on my journey. At my side and sometimes my goad is my wife of 25 years, Kelly. She has encouraged, prodded, corrected and generally been a protector and guard. I am who I am today in part due to her.

Others who have generally been a part of this journey, supporting, pushing and challenging me are many. Names that immediately come to mind for their contributions include, Al, Travis, Lane, Connie, Courtney, Nick, Paulette, Vicky, Karen, Peter, Peter, James, Julian, Chris, Tom, Andres, Tommy, Dorothy, and my mother, Pam Rambo. Each has contributed in various ways that led to growth and further digging into the Word of God and the history of the Christian Church. I am indebted to each of these and many more.

I pray our Father bless them and bring each of us to a fuller understanding of His Word, His promises and His expectations.

Peter G. Rambo, Sr.

FOREWORD

One of those monumental ironies of human existence is that even though our Creator is an Unchanging God, we, His creations, change constantly. This should not be a surprise. After all, if His thoughts and His ways are so far above our thoughts and ways, then we should be in a continuous state of change as He transforms us to be more like Him.

That sounds nice in the clinical setting of a Bible study or a counseling session, but it is not so nice in practical application. The process of transformation produces extreme unpleasantness as those who truly want to pursue YHVH begin to shake the comfortable existence of those who merely say they want to pursue Him.

The Bible gives us so many examples. Think of Noah, Abraham, Jacob, Joseph, Moses, and David. Consider the prophets and judges, men and women of God like Deborah, Isaiah, Jeremiah, Hulda, Ezekiel, Daniel, Hosea, and Amos. The Apostolic Writings (New Testament) continue the story of counter-cultural world changers through the accounts of Peter, Paul, and Stephen.

We consider these people giants of the faith, and indeed they are, although in truth they were no different than the rest of us limited, fallible human beings. What makes them different is that they *believed* God; they took Him at His word and did what He asked of them, expecting that He would fulfill His promises. In the process, they dragged the rest of humanity along with them – that majority who was comfortable with what they had received from ages past, even though it did not match what they knew of the Almighty and His intent to have a people set apart for Himself as His co-regents on this earth.

It does not end there. Several hundred years ago, certain people in Europe began to question the received knowledge that shaped their world. Some of them, like Jan Hus, learned that the simple act of questioning required them to pay the ultimate price. Others, like Martin Luther and John Calvin, prevailed in the face of tremendous opposition, emerging as leaders in what became a global movement of Reformation.

What were they reforming? Certainly not God and His ways, but the way in which He was perceived among their fellow Christians. The European mavericks who lived half a millennium away from us dared to read the Bible for themselves and ask why the people and institutions around them did not conform to what was supposed to be the standard for their existence.

We know what eventually happened, but the people who lived through those tumultuous times did not. None who watched Hus burn at the stake in 1417 could have guessed that one hundred years later Luther would transform the teachings of Hus into a revolution against an all-powerful Catholic hierarchy that had repressed dissent for a thousand years.

And yet the Reformation was not complete. That, too, is a testimony to the unchanging nature of God, and the great distance that separates humanity from Him. The Reformers could bring Christendom giant steps closer to the life of righteousness in faith proclaimed in God's Word, but their own prejudices, shortcomings, frailties – in short, their *humanness* – ensure that they could not complete the journey in their time.

The Reformation was but the next milestone in this 7,000 year plan of YHVH to redeem, restore, and transform humanity into what He had intended all along. It was not the end of the journey by any means, but an essential step that opened the way for centuries of Scriptural inquiry and social change. Generations of Believers took to heart the central lesson of the Reformation: that mankind was not to conform the Word of God to their own version of reality, but instead transform their lives and their communities into something closer to the unchanging standards of the Word.

The work of reformation continues in our time. We have arrived at another milestone: the Torah Awakening which takes this process to what may be the logical conclusion. The question asked is the same as that which Luther and Hus asked.

In fact, it is the same question asked by Yeshua, Peter and Paul; by Amos, Daniel, and Isaiah; by David, Moses, and Abraham: why do the people of the Unchanging God not live according to His revealed Word?

Pete Rambo is among a growing number of disciples of Yeshua who are asking that question and finding answers for our time. The answers are in the place they have always been, hidden in plain sight in the Word of God. What has hidden them from Christian eyes until this generation is the misperception that they applied only to the Jewish people.

According to this reasoning, when Jesus Christ completed His work on the cross, everything changed. The Law (Torah) given by YHVH to Moses no longer applied to those who believed by faith in Jesus and appropriated the salvation offered freely to all people. Everything from Adam to Jesus was cast out, leaving Christians to establish new standards based on the examples of the apostles.

But is that really the case? Did the Unchanging God really change the covenant sign of Sabbath (Shabbat), or the eternal Appointed Times (Feasts) around which the calendar He established revolves? Could it really be true that these "Jewish" practices, which Yeshua and the apostles all followed, still have some application to Believers to this day?

The answer, according to Pete and to many, many others around the world, is "Yes!"

Not only are they applicable, they are the source of great blessing. The people of God are always blessed when they demonstrate their love for Him by doing as He says. Until now, however, we have been hindered in our obedience by an inherited worldview that says Christians should not do what Jews do because anything from Judaism is legalistic, burdensome, and superseded.

That worldview informed Pete's performance of his duties as a Presbyterian pastor. He will tell you that he was not looking to change anything about his life, his denomination, or about Christianity in general. But then something happened: the Holy Spirit began to invite him to look more closely into what he believed, and evaluate that against the full testimony of Scripture. In that sense, he was following in the footsteps of those same giants of the faith, from Abraham to Calvin and Luther. The result was the same: a shattered paradigm and a new journey of discovery into a greater understanding of the Unchanging God.

The journey is not over by any means. In fact, Pete would say it has barely begun. In the pages that follow, he shares the initial steps of this journey through excerpts from his blog, natsab.

If you are on the same journey, or if you are thinking about whether the journey is for you, this book will help. Pete asks the same questions you have asked, or will ask. He shares the answers he has found, and he does so not to define a new, inviolate truth. Rather, he hopes to help his readers shape for themselves a clearer understanding of the Unchanging God.

That, of course, is the point of the entire 7,000 year Divine Experiment. There is a breach between humanity and our Unchanging Creator. Each generation has the potential to close a little more of that breach. Pete Rambo is among those who are doing so in our generation. Read along and find out how.

Albert J. McCarn
Executive Director
B'ney Yosef North America
Charlotte, North Carolina
December 8, 2016

1 RESTORATION!!

I enjoyed collecting badges, particularly in the military. Now, I am not talking about unit patches or crests, rather, I am talking about skill badges that could only be worn after graduating from specialized U. S. Army schools.

As an ROTC Cadet in college, I was favored enough to attend both Airborne and Air Assault Schools, a fairly rare score even for active duty soldiers. Once on active duty, I was blessed to earn the Expert Field Medical Badge and later, due to deployment for Desert Shield/Desert Storm, the Combat Medical Badge. A Ranger Tab was added a bit later.

Earning each of those awards required overcoming physical and/or mental challenges, something that has always appealed to me. The end result was not only being qualified with a particular skill set, but also having a decoration for my uniform and an additional qualifier on my military resume.

Today, all those awards and a dollar won't get me a cup of coffee. Indeed, like most all of the things of this world, they will be destroyed by fire.

There is an award today that I aspire to that will last for all eternity. Hopefully, this is something that excites you as well!

Isaiah 58:12
And your ancient ruins shall be rebuilt; you shall raise up the foundations of many generations; you shall be called the repairer of the breach, the restorer of streets to dwell in.

Can you imagine, for all eternity, being known as one who was a repairer of the breach, a restorer of streets to dwell in? That sounds like an award worthy of pursuing! Today, there are many across the world who, unbeknownst to them, were called to this very purpose as prophecy is unfolding and being fulfilled before our very eyes.

We'll talk more about the above verse and related context later, but here are related verses worth considering,

Amos 9:9-15
"For behold, I will command, and **shake the house of Israel among all the nations** as one shakes with a sieve, but no pebble shall fall to the earth. All the sinners of my people shall die by the sword, who say, 'Disaster shall not overtake or meet us.' "In that day **I will raise up the booth of David** that is fallen and **repair its breaches, and raise up its ruins and rebuild it** as in the days of old, that they may possess the remnant of Edom and all the nations who are called by my name," declares the LORD who does this.
"Behold, the days are coming," declares the LORD, "when the plowman shall overtake the reaper and the treader of grapes him who sows the seed; the mountains shall drip sweet wine, and all the hills shall flow with it. I will restore the fortunes of my people Israel, and they **shall rebuild the ruined cities and inhabit them**; they shall plant vineyards and drink their wine, and they shall make gardens and eat their fruit. I will plant them on their land, and they shall never again be uprooted out of the land that I have given them," says the LORD your God.

These verses point to the latter days, the time I believe we are living in right now.

I have always been interested in prophecy and the study of end times. For two decades I studied and learned as much as I could about the New World Order. I had loads of information and had a good general idea, but never could get it all to fit together completely.

One day, about six years ago, I was sitting at my desk watching YouTube videos in my spare time when, in frustration, I cried out to God, "You gotta show me how all of this fits together!! I can't figure it out!"

He did not answer audibly, but in my spirit I sensed Him direct me down a different path that began a journey of answers instead of questions. I sensed God directing me to begin researching false traditions in Christianity.

Now, understand, I was raised in the Church by missionary parents and was an ordained Presbyterian minister with about eight years in the pulpit. Researching Christian tradition was not an easy thing to do, yet I was on a quest for truth, no matter the cost. I had come to a place where I was willing to pay any price and shed any encumbrance.

My research began with the traditional elements of Christmas and Easter, both of which I shockingly found to precede Christ by more than 500 years. I was especially surprised when I found that the early Apostolic Church celebrated neither, but had a very different form of practice, and that became my real curiosity.

How did the Body in Acts actually practice their faith? What did the disciples DO? When did the Church really begin, and where? How have things changed, and why?

After more than a year of investigating and experiencing increasing blessings and peace as a result of learning and walking in The Way, as the Apostles called it, I began a blog, natsab.com, to share what I was learning.

If you are reading this book, there is a good chance you are asking similar questions or desire truth from God's Word. Maybe, like me, you are questioning the traditions we inherited. I encourage you to walk with me as I share some of those blog posts in an ordered fashion to expose some of those traditions and doctrines that we need to re-evaluate in order to restore the ancient ruins and repair the breach. In doing so, we each help to restore the fallen tent of David. (Amos 9:11ff; Acts 15:15ff; Acts 1:6ff)

I pray one day, together, we can stand before the Lion of the Tribe of Judah and be recognized as Repairers of the Breach!

Each chapter will have a short introduction followed by a group of blog posts on a related topic. You will find that each, some shorter, some longer, is good bubble gum for the brain as challenging topics and subjects are considered and held to the Light of Scripture. Many of these missives you will come back to again and again as you assemble for yourself the pieces of Truth and you find that ALL Scripture fits together and does not need to be explained away or somehow ignored.

May our Father bless you as you set out on this journey, a quest for truth.

2 REFORMATION!!

Early in my journey, I began writing a series of blog posts titled RT for 'Reformation Thought.' Having been reared in the Reformed Presbyterian tradition, I believed that the Reformers had accomplished and arrived at the correct understanding of Scripture. Yet, after eight years as a seminary-trained ordained pastor in the pulpit of a conservative Presbyterian denomination, the Holy Spirit began to ask me questions that exposed me to the reality that there was and is much more in the Christian faith that needs reforming in order to bring it into alignment with the Scriptures.

Following is a series of blog posts I published in early 2013 as I began to share truths the Holy Spirit had been teaching me. Each of these Reformation Thoughts will challenge you. I pray you take the time to ponder each and consider the significance of even the little things in your faith and walk.

RT: Names

Originally posted on January 23, 2013.

We sing, "Blessed be the **name** of the Lord..."

We pray, "..hallowed be Your **name**..."

We say, "The **name** of the Lord is a strong tower..."

His name. I'm sure I never really understood how very important His name is, until recently. Yet there are literally hundreds of verses of Scripture pointing to the significance of His name. How is it that I could go for decades and NOT understand the significance?

Interestingly, the second book of the Bible is called Shemot, a Hebrew word meaning 'names.' In this book we are introduced to a number of players in the grand plan of our Father, but Shemot (Exodus) 3:15 introduces us to the most important!

Exodus 3:15
God, furthermore, said to Moses, "Thus you shall say to the sons of Israel, 'The Lord, the God of your fathers, the God of Abraham, the God of Isaac, and the God of Jacob, has sent me to you.' This is My name forever, and this is My memorial-name to all generations."

I read that in English and say, "No wonder! I don't know His name because the text doesn't say it!"

The Hebrew text says (simply inserting the proper name into the NASB translation), "God, furthermore, said to Moses, "Thus you shall say to the sons of Israel, '**Yahweh**, the God of your fathers, the God of Abraham, the God of Isaac, and the God of Jacob, has sent me to you.' This is My name forever, and this is My memorial-name to all generations."

This verse clearly says, 'This is My name forever, and this is My memorial-name to all generations.'

Most translations use 'God' (class of being) and LORD (title) but never use His proper name.

So why do the English translations use (capital) LORD instead of His proper name?

The simple answer is, the Jewish Rabbis were overzealous in protecting the Name and we have continued to this very day in their error. See, during and after the Babylonian exile, in an effort to make sure Judah did not break Yahweh's commandments and again cause Him to bring judgment, they erected fences around the Law. In this case, they ceased to say the name of Yahweh and began substituting the word Adonai (Lord) in its place when reading or saying any piece of Scripture. (Matthew 15:2 and following explain how Jesus handled a similar 'fence.') The rabbis meant well, but in doing so, violated the very Word of Yahweh in Exodus 3:15. Not good! We are told in Exodus 20:7, among other places, not to take His name in vain, or not to make it common. Nowhere are we ever told not to use His name. Yet, that is just what they did, and what we have learned, by tradition, to do.

Instead of 'Yahweh' in the nearly 7000(!) places His name appears in the Hebrew text, we find 'LORD' or occasionally 'GOD.'

Interestingly, most all good study Bibles have the name 'Yahweh' (or, 'Yehovah') printed right in them, but not between Genesis 1:1 and Revelation 22:21. Yep, you guessed it. The publisher's notes or Foreword tells you, in more detail, exactly what I just wrote.

Read and absorb the following verses with His proper name. Marinate in the significance of knowing His proper name. See each verse in context ... even begin to read your Bible and mentally say His proper name each time you see 'LORD.' At first it may seem hokey, but if you will do it, I guarantee you will be blessed beyond what you can imagine. His name truly is wonderful.

Jeremiah 16:21

Therefore behold, I am going to make them know— this time I will make them know My power and My might; and they shall know that My **name** is **Yahweh.**

Isaiah 42:8
I am **Yahweh**, that is My **name**; I will not give My glory to another, nor My praise to graven images.

Hosea 12:5
Even **Yahweh** Tzevaoth, **Yahweh** is His **name.**

Amos 5:8
He who made the Pleiades and Orion and changes deep darkness into morning, Who also darkens day into night, Who calls for the waters of the sea and pours them out on the surface of the earth, **Yahweh** is His **name.**

Joel 2:32
And it will come about that whoever calls on the **name** of **Yahweh** will be delivered; For on Mount Zion and in Jerusalem there will be those who escape, as **Yahweh** has said, even among the survivors whom **Yahweh** calls.

Zechariah 13:9
And I will bring the third part through the fire, refine them as silver is refined, and test them as gold is tested. They will call on My **name**, and I will answer them; I will say, 'They are My people,' and they will say, '**Yahweh** is my God.'"

And here is an interesting one....

Matthew 23:39
For I say to you, from now on you will not see Me until you say, 'BLESSED IS HE WHO COMES IN THE **NAME** OF **YAHWEH**!'

Seems pretty important to the King of Kings! If we want to see Him, maybe we should learn His Father's name!

8

We can save the name of Jesus for a later date. But here's a hint: There is no letter 'J' or 'J' sound in Hebrew or Greek. Even in Latin, there is no 'J' sound. That showed up around the 12th century. Just a thought.

The Reformation is only beginning. We must seek to worship in spirit and truth.

In Hebrew, the name of God is יהוה or, YHWH referred to as the Tetragrammaton. No one, and I mean NO ONE, knows precisely how to correctly pronounce this, though closest educated assumptions are 'Yahweh' or 'Yehovah.'

Today, I prefer Yehovah to Yahweh, but both are acceptable. Certainly, a difference in understanding how to pronounce the Name should NOT bring division. Rather, I believe our Father in Heaven just appreciates the fact that like little children learning to talk, we are trying to honor Him by referring to Him rightly, even if imperfectly.

RT: Olam!

Originally posted on January 23, 2013.

I distinctly remember a gathering in late November of 2011 at Mr. and Mrs. Caldwell's home right up the road from us. It was a balmy Sunday afternoon with a short but torrential thunderstorm that threatened to dampen the jovial occasion until the low sun in the west broke through and chased the dark clouds from the sky.

As it did so, a brilliant rainbow was emblazoned on the dark receding clouds across Newberry Road capped with a fainter, but very visible, second rainbow. As most parents have at one time or another, I grabbed the teachable moment and draped my arm across the shoulders of one of my growing boys.

"That's beautiful, isn't it?"

"Yeah," he responded. We just soaked in the moment and the incredible contrast of storm and rainbow. Certainly, it was one of the prettier ones I have seen.

"You know what that means, right?" Of course he knew, but the question gets asked every time we see a rainbow. How can it not be asked? It is one of those 'forever' promises that we have from our Father in heaven, and every time He displays a rainbow it is intended to remind both Him <u>and</u> us that His promise to Noah is forever.

In fact, Yahweh (God) tells Noah 'Olam!' twice in the Genesis 9 recounting. Verse 12 says, "God said, 'This is the sign of the covenant which I am making between me and you and every living creature that is with you, for **everlasting (olam)** generations;'" Verse 16 says, "When the bow is in the cloud, then I will look upon it, to remember the **everlasting (olam)** covenant between God and every living creature of all flesh that is on the earth."

Recently, I woke in the middle of the night thinking, '**Olam!**' No kidding!

I got out of bed and slipped into the quiet den so I could consider some of the uses of this Hebrew word of promise.

Strongs Concordance points to more than 430 uses of **olam** in the Old Testament with a variety of translational words including 'ages, always, continual, eternal, long, never' and 'permanently,' though most uses fall into three words: 'everlasting (112), forever (206) and perpetual (29).'

There are so many great promises that, like the covenant of the rainbow, are **olam**! **Forever**! **Everlasting**!!

From the previous Reformation Thought: Exodus 3:15 "God, furthermore, said to Moses, "Thus you shall say to the sons of Israel, 'Yahweh . . . is My **name forever (olam)**, and this is my memorial **name** to all generations.'"

Psalm 136 tells us 26 times that 'His lovingkindness is **everlasting (olam)**.'

Psalm 105:8, 10 His covenant is a **forever (olam)** covenant... confirmed to Israel as an **everlasting (olam)** covenant. (See Gen. 17:7-8)

In Isaiah 63:12 speaking of the lovingkindness of Yahweh (v.7) Isaiah says, "Who caused His glorious arm to go at the right hand of Moses, Who divided the waters before them to make for Himself an **everlasting (olam) name**,"

2 Samuel 7:13-16 The Davidic Kingship is promised to be **forever. Olam!** Hallelujah! (See also Ezekiel 37:24-28!! **Olam x 4!!** See them?)

2 Chronicles 7:14-16 Yahweh's **name** is in/on Jerusalem **forever. Olam**!

You get the picture. There are dozens and dozens of similar references.

But, what if **olam** suddenly didn't mean **everlasting** or **forever**? What if Yahweh didn't *really* mean **olam**? What if we could decide what is **olam** and what isn't? Can we? Some doctrines and traditions try. Let's compare to the **olam** (eternal/everlasting) Word.

Leviticus 23:14, 21, 31, 41
[The Feasts of Yahweh] shall be a **perpetual (olam)** statute throughout your generations.

Numbers 15:15-16
As for the assembly [qahal: congregation/church; see Acts 7:38] there shall be one statute for you and for the alien who sojourns with you, a **perpetual (olam)** statute throughout your generations; as you are, so shall the alien be before Yahweh. There is to be one law and one ordinance for you and for the alien who sojourns with you. (Compare with Eph. 4:4-6)

Exodus 31:16-17
So the sons of Israel shall observe the Sabbath, to celebrate the Sabbath throughout their generations as a **perpetual (olam)** covenant. It is a sign between Me and the sons of Israel **forever (olam)**; for in six days Yahweh made heaven and earth, but on the seventh day He ceased and was refreshed.

Psalm 119:44-45
So I will keep Your Torah (law) continually, **forever (olam)** and ever, and I will walk at liberty for I seek Your precepts.

Psalm 119:111-112
I have inherited Your testimonies **forever (olam)**, for they are the joy of my heart. I have inclined my heart to perform Your statutes **forever (olam)**, to the end.

Hmmm... Suddenly the warm fuzzies of the rainbow are gone and **olam** doesn't seem like such an easy word to grapple with.

Does Yahweh *really* mean **forever**? His Word seems to indicate that He does. Consider:

Sabbaths in the Millennium: See in context, Isaiah 66:23. "'And it shall be from new moon to new moon and from Sabbath to Sabbath, all mankind will come to bow down before Me,' says Yahweh."

Feasts in the Millennium: See in context, Zechariah 14:16. "Then it will come about that any who are left of all nations that went up against Jerusalem will go up from year to year to worship the King, Yahweh Tzevaoth, and to celebrate the Feast of Booths." (Feast of Booths also mentioned in verses 18 & 19!!)

Eating unclean in the Millennium: See in context, Isaiah 66:16-17 "For Yahweh will execute judgment by fire and by His sword on all flesh, and those slain by Yahweh will be many. 'Those who sanctify and purify themselves to go to the gardens, following one in the center (pagan rituals?) who eat swine's flesh, detestable things and mice, will come to an end altogether,' declares Yahweh." (see also Isaiah 65:1-7, especially v. 4)

Please understand, I KNOW this is rough sailing in turbulent waters. Doctrines and traditions can become sacred if not held with an open hand. The Word of our God must be the final authority. This trip will get smoother, but we have to address a few more challenging questions.

The Reformation is only beginning. We must seek to worship in spirit and <u>truth.</u>

RT: Grafting

Originally posted on January 23, 2013.

I don't consider myself much of a farmer. Yes, we raise tilapia, have several beehives and half a dozen milk goats. We have laying hens, a greenhouse and raised garden beds. We even have eight or nine fruit trees and a dozen or more fruiting vines. Still, I only reluctantly claim any ability to grow anything. The real reason is that I know I do not have the proverbial 'green thumb.' Just check the spot where I have managed to kill two beautiful apricot trees. It stands as a testament to the many other plants that I have tortured or terminated in any number of dumb ways.

Maybe that is why I consider **grafting** to be one of the so called 'holy grails' of farming. There seems a certain mystery to it, but I aim to learn more about it this year. Someone recently told me of an article about how to **graft** tomato plants for increased yield and multiple varieties on a single vine. Sounds like a new way to destroy formerly green plants that I'm itching to try. But, I digress.

Grafting is indeed a tricky piece of husbandry whereby a branch or bud from one plant or tree can be trimmed and inserted into a notch in a strong(er) plant for the benefit of nourishment from the root stock. The cutting by itself, in most cases, will die. However, if someone who knows what they are doing can trim it up and properly **graft** it into a choice stock/stump, it will bear much fruit.

Paul rightly uses the **grafting** metaphor in Romans 11:17-24 when he explains how Gentiles 'become partakers of the rich root of the olive tree.' At least six times in those eight verses he uses the words **graft** and **grafting**.

I have long understood myself to be a full partaker of the blessings of the covenants through faith in Yeshua/Jesus. He is the rich root (John 15) and Scripture in multiple places identifies

Yahweh as the husbandman. I'm not sure I ever really studied out the fullness or the root of Paul's analogy. (Pun intended... lol!)

Ephesians 2 clearly details that we are now members of the Commonwealth of Israel. Ephesians 4 articulates a lot of 'ones:' one body, one hope, one Lord, one faith, one baptism, etc. Galatians 6:16 calls us the Israel of God.

Somehow in the middle of understanding that I was a full partaker, I had this lingering thought in the back of my head that made me feel like a 'second class' citizen or even a 'redheaded step child.' (Apologies to any redheads...) I guess the reason is because I had never traced the root of Paul's metaphor and understood that he was not teaching anything new. In fact, he was teaching a very old concept.

First, where does Paul get the olive tree part of his metaphor? Ever thought about that? Me neither. Look at Jeremiah 11:16! The sin of the House of Israel and the House of Judah led to Yahweh judging His 'green olive tree' previously 'beautiful in fruit and form.' Here is where Paul gets the idea of branches being broken off for unbelief. (Rom. 11:21-22)

More importantly, where does Paul get the idea of **grafting** in Gentiles? I always thought that his ministry to Gentiles was something new. Yes, I knew Israel had been called as a 'light to the nations' but assumed that they simply had never fulfilled this calling.

If we dig a little deeper, we find that, while Paul did have a specific ministry to the Gentiles, he wasn't doing anything new. Yahweh had made a place for non-Hebrews- often called foreigners, aliens, or sojourners- to be a part of Israel from the very beginning. In fact, Abraham himself was an alien and sojourner when Yahweh called him into relationship, but that is getting ahead the story.

Perhaps the clearest example with which we are all familiar is Ruth. She was a Moabitess who chose to join herself to Naomi and more importantly, Naomi's Elohim (God). Ruth 1:16-17 says,

Ruth 1:16-17
But Ruth said, "Do not urge me to leave you or turn back from following you; for where you go, I will go, and where you lodge, I will lodge. Your people shall be my people, and your God, my God. Where you die, I will die, and there I will be buried. Thus may Yahweh do to me, and worse, if anything but death parts you and me."

Notice that Ruth joined herself to Israel and not the other way around. Not only does she know Yahweh by name, but she understands that she is joining herself to a destiny, a land, a people, and to Yahweh, Naomi's God. She has a very clear understanding of what it means to be **grafted** in. But, where does she get this idea? We keep going back.

A study of Moses reveals literally a couple dozen references to 'the alien who sojourns with you' and 'the foreigner who dwells among you.' Numbers 15:14-16 is a clear example of Yahweh's provision for those who are not of physical Hebrew descent.

Numbers 15:14-16
If an alien sojourns with you, or one who may be among you throughout your generations, and he wishes to make an offering by fire, as a soothing aroma to Yahweh, just as you do so shall he do. As for the assembly (qahal/church), <u>there shall be one statute for you and for the alien who sojourns with you</u>, a perpetual (olam) statute throughout your generations; as you are, so shall the alien be before Yahweh. There is to be one law (Torah) and one ordinance for you and for the alien who sojourns with you.

Exodus 12:49 echoes almost verbatim,

Exodus 12:49

16

The same law (Torah) shall apply to the native as to the stranger who sojourns among you.

We should not be surprised at Yahweh's provision for the alien who sojourned. In fact, many non-Hebrews had apparently partaken of Passover. They had entered under the blood of the Lamb, passed through the waters of the Red Sea and come to the base of Sinai to hear the expectations of proper obedience as a response to Yahweh's loving salvation. Exodus 12:38 tells us that *"a mixed multitude also went up with them."* Here is the first major example of **grafting** in, though we could go further back to Tamar (Gen. 38) or even to the calling out of Abraham who was the first Ivri (Hebrew, meaning 'crossed over').

When Paul teaches that all who are of the spiritual seed of Abraham (Romans 9:6-8) are children of the promise and therefore regarded as descendants we understand what Ruth understood. Like her, when we place faith and trust in Messiah, we are **grafted** in and no longer identify ourselves as outsiders or even Gentiles, but as members of the Commonwealth of Israel. We are recipients of the promises that include a destiny, a land, and a people in addition to being, like Abraham, called a friend of God (James 2:23; 4:4). There is no difference in Jew or Greek, we are all one in Messiah. The yet unfulfilled promises to Israel involving land, destiny and kingdom, both physical and spiritual, belong to all who believe. Ezekiel 37:24-28 speaks of all who are **grafted** in having One shepherd with one statute (Law) residing in the land forever. We are the dry bones that will yet live again (Ez.37:11-14), one of the two sticks joined in His hand (Ez. 37:19)! (See Ez. 36 & 37 for larger context.)

If we are **grafted** in, then we are not a separate plan, or a second option. Yeshua Messiah's ministry was one of propitiation and restoration as he reconciles us to Yahweh that we might walk in obedience to the fullness of what it means to be His chosen people, a holy nation, and a royal priesthood. We are grafted into the rich Root of Israel.

An important closing point is that **we do not replace Israel.** *We are joined to Israel!* Like Ruth, we are grafted to a destiny, a people, a land and to Yahweh, Elohenu Melech ha'olam! (Yahweh our God, King of the Universe.)

If you want to study more about who we are in Messiah, here is a terrific teaching that digs out many Scriptures identifying and explaining Israel's prophecy over Manasseh and Ephraim: http://119ministries.com/the-lost-sheep

The Reformation is only beginning. We must seek to worship in spirit and truth.

RT: Manipulatives

Originally posted on January 28, 2013.

Neither my wife, nor I, ever planned to be educators. Certainly, parenting has an inherent requirement involving education as we 'train up our children,' but homeschooling was not our expectation when we began some six or more years ago. During that time-frame I think we have learned more about education and how to educate than we ever expected. If anything, we are the ones getting an education.

One interesting concept I had never considered was the developmental thought process of a child, particularly in the area of math. In the earliest stages of mental development and awareness, a child can only deal with concrete items. Abstract concepts are so foreign that they cannot process or grasp them.

An example is how children are taught to count. Universally, parents use concrete items like fingers, blocks, Cheerios, etc. Just look in any kindergarten classroom and see the plethora of toys that are designed to engage the child on a concrete level. They can manipulate these items and through the physical, begin to grasp principles that will later enable and enhance their abstract thinking skills.

A couple of our boys struggled with math, so we chose a program called *Math-U-See* to help in learning the basic skills using manipulatives. The interactive nature of the concrete objects helped and continue to help them in understanding concepts, even as they mature into adolescents capable of abstract thought.

About a month ago, during our celebration of Hanukkah, it dawned on me that Yahweh (God) knew exactly what He was doing when He instituted His special feast days. He was instituting manipulatives that would teach us and help us teach our children about Himself and His plan for history and Redemption. While Hanukkah is not one of the seven major feasts instituted by Yahweh in Leviticus 23, the lesson of manipulatives was not lost on me.

All of Scripture uses direct lessons, metaphors and allusions to the created order and the times and seasons instituted by Yahweh to teach and draw us nearer to Him. As early as Genesis 1:14 we are told that Yahweh's creation has a purpose to teach and lead us to Him. "Then God said, "Let there be lights in the expanse of the heavens to separate the day from the night, and let them be for signs and for seasons (H4150: moed) and for days and years;"

According to Strong's Concordance, 'moed' means 'appointed time, place or meeting.' 'Seasons,' as it appears in Genesis 1:14 is in keeping with the nature of 'appointed times.' More significantly, it is Yahweh's time and beyond our ability to change or ignore... but we won't go that route today.

In Leviticus 23 we are told at least five times that Yahweh has appointed a particular feast (moed) or time for a holy convocation. Why? For what purpose?

In pondering this I think in His infinite wisdom, He understands our frame and our needs. Let me explain.

We are charged with training up our children in the way they should go. Deuteronomy 6:4-9 articulates the continual nature of our task to teach and even alludes to manipulatives in terms of times ('when you rise up'), places ('in the way') and objects ('hand, eyes, door').

More significantly, nowhere in Scripture are we ever referred to as the 'adults of God.' In fact, quite the opposite. Over and over Scripture calls us the 'children of God' or teaches and treats us as children. We are continually called to run to Him as a child to his father. We are portrayed as fickle and without sense apart from Him and His ways. Perhaps that is why He gave us so many manipulatives to continually draw our attention back to Him and through which He can teach new truths.

So, why does Christendom tend to eschew manipulatives? Why do we particularly ignore feasts, fasts, and dietary instructions from our Creator?

The answer, I believe, is in the gnostic influences present in the early church. Gnosticism, a Greek thought process that pre-dated Yeshua by a couple hundred years, teaches, among other things, that the spiritual world is superior to the physical world. Through absorbing some of the Gnostic heresy of abasing the physical while focusing on the spiritual leads directly to the elimination of the very manipulatives Yahweh instituted and commanded to be kept forever (see RT: Olam!). His design is to give us physical, tangible reminders through which we can learn and teach our children, thus being obedient on a number of levels.

In fact, I believe we cannot fully learn and understand most abstract concepts without some concrete basis to work from. Thus, the Feasts of Yahweh are significant!

My family and I are neophytes as we have only enjoyed the Feasts for the last two years. However, I continually hear from those who have been on this Hebraic walk for 10, 15, even 20 years that with every feast they learn something new! No wonder Rav Shaul (Paul) tells us in 1 Corinthians 5:8, "therefore let us celebrate the feast," and in Colossians 2:17 that the Feasts are "shadows of good things to come!" See? They are instructive and point us toward yet future goodness that is embodied in Yeshua Messiah!

Both of these letters are written long after the death, burial and resurrection of Messiah, yet Shaul says, "Keep them!" Further, his example in the Book of Acts is the keeping of the feasts and the rest of the Torah. (See Acts 15:20-21; 20:6, 16; 21:21-26; 24:13-15; 25:7-11; 28:17-18; as well as a dozen or more references to him teaching and preaching on the Sabbath to both Jew and Greek.)

So, before I head off on a tangent, here is the point: Yahweh has given us manipulatives for our benefit and for that of our children as we train them up: His Feasts, fasts, dietary instructions, etc. Why do we ignore them? Why would we want to? They are for our benefit and His greater glory!

The next Reformation Thought will be a fun one! It will be a chance for deep introspection for all of us. Consider: Anti-Semitism.

May our King grant you His everlasting peace!

RT: Anti-Semitism

Originally posted on February 5, 2013.

RT: Anti-Semitism, or *The Confessions of a Misguided Pastor*

If our doctrine prevented millions of Jews from knowing their Jewish Messiah, would we care? Should we?

I have really tried to figure out some hook to start this post, but nothing comes. All I have is a broken heart and the horribly sick sensation that I have utterly failed my Messiah. When I stop and ponder the subject of **anti-Semitism** and my role in promoting such, I am physically ill. Maybe I feel just a little like Rav Shaul (the apostle Paul) felt as he was led by the hand to the house of Judas in Damascus. He could neither eat or drink he was so sick of heart. In fact, I believe that ill feeling would haunt him the rest of his life, driving him to the lengths he was willing to go as a bond servant of Yeshua.

Shaul had not recognized the Messiah in the day of His visitation. In fact, he had gone so far as to persecute those who had, even assisting in the putting to death of Stephen. Now, Yeshua haMashiach (Jesus the Messiah) had revealed Himself in truth and glory on the road to Damascus and Shaul was sick. Beyond sick. He was shattered.

How could this have happened? How could he, a Pharisees of Pharisees, one who knew the Tanak (Old Testament) forwards and backwards, one who was a rising star among the leaders of Judaism, be so terribly wrong? He was sick! Utterly broken.

Shaul had been a faithful student who passionately sought Yahweh. He had played by the rules, only to find out the playbook he was using was not that of Yahweh. He had made the critical mistake of trusting the ages old playbook, *Doctrine and Tradition.*

I grew up by that playbook. Those who taught me meant well. I learned all the lines, had the prooftexts and could recite the lines of respected 'church fathers.' I graduated from a good seminary where well-meaning men taught me to 'defend my faith' and 'preach the Gospel.' I pastored a church for ten years and taught zealously the 'doctrines of grace.'

Yet, here I sit. Broken. Moved to tears when I ponder the gravity of what I have done and how I have hurt the heart of my Messiah. How did it ever come to this?

During my army days, after training exercises, we would have introspective 'AARs,' or, After Action Reviews. Like FAA inspectors after an airplane crash, we would look at every detail of the operation/exercise to try to determine what went right and what went wrong. What root causes contributed to the disaster. How could we repair the damage or insure not to make the same mistake again.

I have done much the same in trying to understand the contributing factors to this great ache in my soul. How did I get here? What went wrong? How do I insure this never happens again? I have hurt my King and taught/encouraged others to do the same!

What is this great pain I have inflicted upon Him? I have promoted **anti-Semitism**. I spent years of my life teaching against and, by example, denying the very Word of our Lord. Oh, I professed a love for Israel, and prayed often for the peace of Yerushlayim (Jerusalem), but my teaching and actions belied something very different without me even knowing it. I denied my Messiah and all He stood for.

Complete introspection and detailed analysis of the multiple ways would fill several books, so this will be a brief, but I pray, a very challenging overview of the AAR. Please walk with me here as I confess and recount some of the ways I denied my Savior before I explain how/why I committed these abominable acts.

I celebrated Christmas and Easter, holidays rooted in paganism. Just look in any encyclopedia. I may have meant well, yet, Deuteronomy 12: 29-32 among other passages clearly tells us that syncretism is an abomination to Yahweh. Inexcusable. (For more information, see: http://119ministries.com/sunburned-part-1)

I ignored the dietary instructions of clean and unclean and taught these to be abrogated (Westminster Confession of Faith WCF. XIX, iii) contrary to clear Scripture from the mouth of my Messiah (Matthew 5:17-19).

I worshiped on Sunday according to the doctrines of men (WCF. XXI, vii), but contrary to the everlasting commandment (Exodus 31:12-17).

I ignored the Feasts of Yahweh, contrary to the everlasting covenant (see RT: Olam!), while teaching that these were done away with (WCF. XIX, iii), despite Scripture to the contrary (Zech. 14:16-19).

I called Yeshua by a Greek name, 'Jesus,' thus denying, with each use, His real heritage and even who He is. Yeshua means 'salvation, deliverer.' What does Jesus mean? There isn't even a letter 'J' or 'j' sound in the Hebrew alephbet (alphabet) or even in Greek!

Probably the most egregious was maintaining and promoting the idea that the church IS Israel, though I was careful to avoid the idea that we *replaced* Israel, either idea being a far cry from the truth of being grafted INTO Israel. In conjunction with this horrid error, I believed that for those of Jewish descent to be saved they had to come to 'our' Messiah instead of us going to them and 'their' Messiah. (I never really pondered the fact that Yeshua haMashiach/Jesus the Messiah was a Sabbath keeping, feast observing, kosher eating, tassel wearing Jew!)

There are many other evidences, but these are damning enough to prove beyond any shadow of doubt that I lived and promoted **anti-Semitism**.

How so? Multiple ways, actually.

Denying the commandments is denying my Messiah. It denies His very essence, who He is, the Word made flesh, as well as denying how and through whom He chose to reveal Himself. Doing so is **anti-Semitic** at its root.

Teaching that my Messiah taught or even endorsed the errors I walked in has the effect of <u>forcing</u> the Jews to NOT believe in Him. Further, they are commanded to stone (or, in modern times they shun) any who might convert to Jesus. Yep, you read that right. Deuteronomy 13 commands that *anyone* who teaches or presents a Messiah contrary to Torah is to be separated from Israel. Just take the <u>Deuteronomy 13 Test</u> (http://119ministries.com/the-deuteronomy-13-test). See? Preaching a seemingly non-Jewish Messiah is **anti-Semitism** by removing from the Jews their own Messiah. Further, it is the act of preaching a false gospel and a false Messiah.

Teaching, or even hinting that the church somehow replaced Israel has the effect of denying the very tree into which <u>I am grafted</u>. Replacing Israel IS **anti-Semitism**. Overt dispensationalism (Baptist/Arminian) or covert dispensationalism (Presbyterian/Lutheran/Reformed) is still **anti-Semitism**.

Changing the name of Yeshua to Jesus denies His Jewishness and is **anti-Semitic** to the core. Think about it.

There are more ways to be very 'religious' and hide **anti-Semitism**, but we'll move on. How did I get this way? Was I far afield of that which my denomination taught? Had I cast off everything I had been taught in a conservative seminary? Was I some closet radical who sought to undermine Messiah, or was I blindly following traditions?

While I have no excuse and am totally accountable for my actions, I was simply following what I had been taught. The doctrines and traditions of men that I had accepted were deeply influenced by **anti-Semitism.**

Consider what I had accepted. The doctrines and traditions I had embraced were either directly from or heavily influenced by:

Martin Luther:
> What shall we Christians do with this rejected and condemned people, the Jews? . . . First, to set fire to their synagogues or schools and to bury and cover with dirt whatever will not burn. . . . Second, I advise that their houses also be razed and destroyed. . . . Third, I advise that all their prayer books and Talmudic writings, in which such idolatry, lies, cursing, and blasphemy are taught, be taken from them. . . . Fourth, I advise that their rabbis be forbidden to teach henceforth on pain of loss of life and limb. . . . Fifth, I advise that safe-conduct on the highways be abolished completely for the Jews. . . . Sixth, I advise that usury be prohibited to them, and that all cash and treasure of silver and gold be taken from them. . . . Seventh, I recommend putting a flail, an ax, a hoe, a spade, a distaff, or a spindle into the hands of young, strong Jews and Jewesses and letting them earn their bread in the sweat of their brow, as was imposed on the children of Adam. . . .(Martin Luther, *On the Jews and Their Lies*, 1543.)

John Calvin: (Though Calvin was not enamored with Luther's well known tirade, he was no angel.)
> Their [the Jews] rotten and unbending stiffneckedness deserves that they be oppressed unendingly and without measure or end and that they die in their misery without the pity of anyone." (John Calvin, "Ad Quaelstiones et Objecta Juaei Cuiusdam Responsio" (A Response To Questions and Objections of a Certain Jew), in Gerhard Falk, *The Jew in Christian Theology* (London: McFarland & Co., 1931).)

Roman Catholic Church:

Multiple church fathers quoted at http://www.yashanet.com/library/fathers.htm

These are but a very small collection as mere examples of the attitude of the Roman Catholic Church toward Jews. Add to that the pogroms in the name of Jesus.

Remember, Luther, Calvin and the Roman Catholic fathers quoted above either wrote or were heavily influential in the very basic tenets of all doctrine taught in the church today. The attitudes presented here are like a poison that permeates every doctrine. Therefore, everything taught or opined that touches on all things Jewish or Hebrew must be re-evaluated. Yes, they had much right, but clearly, they had much wrong! In light of the foul stench of **anti-Semitism**, every doctrine of Christianity, must be re-evaluated from the foundation of the Word.

But it wasn't just the church that got us here. Consider:

Constantine:

> On the Venerable Day of the Sun [*venerabili die Solis*— the sacred day of the Sun] let the magistrates and people residing in cities rest, and let all workshops be closed. In the country, however, persons engaged in agriculture may freely and lawfully continue their pursuits; because it often happens that another day is not so suitable for grain-sowing or for vine-planting; lest by neglecting the proper moment for such operations the bounty of heaven should be lost. (Given the 7th day of March, [A.D. 321], Crispus and Constantine being consuls each of them for the second time.) (The First Sunday Law of Constantine, in *Codex Justinianus*, lib. 3, tit. 12, 3; trans. in Phillip Schaff *History of the Christian Church*, Vol. 3, p. 380.)

Deeper research reveals that in the second century the newborn sect of Judaism called simply The Way by some adherents and Notzrim (Hebrew for 'The Branch,' likely mistranslated as 'Nazarenes') by some detractors had been all but taken over by Greek bishops with a radically different mindset and an arrogant attitude of superiority. Steeped in Western Hellenist thought, they began to erase the Eastern Hebrew mindset and methods of Scriptural understanding and interpretation. Add to this the growing hatred of the Jews in that day due to their unwillingness to bow to Rome and a heady mix was born. The Jewish Pharisees were trying to sever any ties with the upstart exponentially growing Gentile followers of Messiah while Rome was battling for the survival of their empire and they demanded the allegiance of all.

Bottom line, I believe Constantine saw an opportunity to create an empty shell that he could then fill as he saw fit for the future of his kingdom. With a new alliance with the bishop of Rome, he created an environment whereby the beginnings of the Roman Catholic Church could meld paganism and twisted belief in Messiah resulting in a syncretistic mixture of Hebrew-less Scripture and pagan practices.

The resulting mixture of **anti-Semitism** effectively obliterated the Hebrew roots of what we call the Christian faith. The church today, through inherited but well-hidden **anti-Semitism**, has created a different religion instead of the faith of our fathers Abraham, Isaac and Jacob.

[Aside: I do believe there is much grace from our Father for those who believed and worshipped in ignorance, however, I am no longer ignorant and am accountable for what I have learned. If you have read this far, you are also accountable!]

I have no excuse and hold no one other than myself accountable for my teaching and acceptance of false traditions. I blame only myself and confess openly that I was horribly wrong. My heart aches, as I pray yours does too. 2 Chronicles 7:13-16 comes to mind.

I am not alone in coming to this understanding. It is part of a growing awakening that is occurring all over the planet because of the ready availability of truth on the internet. Those who seek truth are researching and finding the very things I have found.

Interestingly, in the last decade there has been a growing movement of recognition of this theft of our heritage and inheritance. It is a fulfillment of Yermiyahu (Jeremiah) 16:19-21.

Jeremiah 16:19-21
O Yahweh, my strength and my stronghold,
And my refuge in the day of distress,
To You the nations will come
From the ends of the earth and say,
"Our fathers have inherited nothing but falsehood,
Futility and things of no profit."
Can man make gods for himself?
Yet they are not gods!
"Therefore behold, I am going to make them know—
This time I will make them know
My power and My might;
And **they shall know that My name is Yahweh."**

Why now? What makes our generation special in that we suddenly begin to understand something even the Reformation fathers did not see? I can't answer that other than to quote Scripture and bask in the humbling honor that Abba has bestowed on us with His visitation.

Malachi 4 is future prophecy. Read carefully and ponder what the prophet tells us:

Malachi 4:1-6
For behold, the day is coming, burning like a furnace; and **all the arrogant and every evildoer** will be chaff; and the day that is coming will set them ablaze," says Yahweh Tzevaoth, "so that it will leave them neither root nor branch." But for **you who fear My name**, the sun of righteousness will rise with healing in its wings; and you will go forth and skip about like calves from the stall. You will tread down the wicked, for they will be ashes under the soles of your feet on the day which I am preparing," says Yahweh Tzevaoth.

"**Remember the law of Moshe** My servant, *even the* statutes and ordinances which I commanded him in Horeb for **all** Israel.

"Behold, I am going to send you **Elijah the prophet before the coming of the great and terrible day of Yahweh.** He will restore the hearts of the fathers to *their* children and the hearts of the children to their fathers, so that I will not come and smite the land with a curse."

My fathers are Abraham, Isaac and Jacob, not Luther, Calvin or Knox. My heritage is Hebrew, not Roman Catholic pagan Hellenism. My future is the Messianic Kingdom in Israel for the Millennial reign and then the New Heaven and New earth, not some ethereal non-descript heaven.

I pray you understand my ache, and awakening to truth. Further, I pray that Yahweh open your eyes and break your heart as you see Yeshua haMashiach, the Lion of the tribe of JUDAH who is regathering the Lost Sheep!

It will take you a long time to process all of the info in this post and as I stated early on, this is a mere overview. I encourage you to read or watch all of the links in this post. Get out your Bible and dig through it. If you are near me, come sit down and let's reason together, swap questions, and spend time before our Father and ask Him to reveal truth! He forgives and is waiting for you to come to fullness of the knowledge of Him and who He called you to be.

Embrace your heritage and waste not another day in the false doctrines of men!

The Reformation is just beginning!

RT: Riches

Originally posted on February 11, 2013.

As a young teen I did lots of odd jobs to make a little spending money. These varied from the mundane babysitting and lawn cutting to cleaning old bricks.

A gentleman in the community who was building a house wanted a bunch of old bricks for his new chimney and fireplace, so he offered me a penny or maybe two cents for every brick from a preexisting structure that I could clean. The result was that word got around and several others had me perform the same job for them.

The cleaning basically involved a mortar hammer and a cold chisel to cut the bricks from rubble and then to chip off any mortar, thus cleaning them up. It was time consuming and difficult work, to say the least. Hours and hours of monotonous work for a 12-13 year old, but it was spending money.

Anyway, as I worked tearing apart and cleaning the bricks from the mantle area of this antiquated chimney, I popped a brick out and found a silver mercury dime! Small treasure for most, but at the time I was learning a little from another local gentleman about coin collecting and it was hard work to make and save the money necessary to purchase additions to my little collection. This was indeed great treasure for me!! I was SO excited! (I did ask the gentleman I was working for if he wanted it and he graciously let me have it.)

I still have that little dime and even now it is probably not worth more than $3, but I distinctly remember the joy over that 'found' treasure that represented about 200 cleaned bricks. Unexpected riches!

Yeshua, in Luke 15, tells a parable saying,
Luke 15:9-10

> Or what woman, having ten silver coins, if she loses one coin, does not light a lamp, sweep the house, and search carefully until she finds *it?* And when she has found *it,* she calls *her* friends and neighbors together, saying, 'Rejoice with me, for I have found the piece which I lost!' Likewise, I say to you, there is joy in the presence of the angels of God over one sinner who repents.

No doubt, thousands of sermons have been preached from this passage about the repenting of a sinner and the value of the coin, etc. Still, recently, something else dawned on me as I pondered this passage.

Was He who said, "if you love Me, keep my commandments" possibly pointing to a deeper meaning? I am finding that most Scripture is like an onion with layers of meaning. Let me postulate a deeper meaning than the surface meaning I have heard countless times.

A woman. How often is the church, or congregation referred to as a woman in Scripture? Often. A possible fit here.

Ten coins. Several 'tens' in Scripture but the first two that come to mind are the ten scattered tribes, but that doesn't seem to fit. The Ten Commandments however, seem a perfect fit. Very valuable. Not lost... well, except one.

The lost coin. Valuable. Worth searching for. Hmmm.... Could it be? The 4th commandment?

The woman, when she has found the coin "calls *her* friends and neighbors together, saying, 'Rejoice with me, for I have found the piece which I lost!'" This is the expected response!

It is interesting to note that over and over I hear from those who 'find' the 4th commandment and the great joy they have. To the consternation of all those around, 'friends and neighbors,' they tell with great zeal of the treasure now back in their possession.

My experience, being no different, has been one of finding great treasure! Found riches of inestimable value! The Feasts of Yahweh have been a wonderful, enriching, physical and instructive experience of my Messiah, Yeshua (Jesus). Further, the blessings of obedience have been innumerable. This was the first of several treasures we found in the last couple years.

Shabbat (Sabbath) was the second of the several riches. What blessings to leave behind the doctrines and traditions of men. Now, I don't have to justify why Scripture doesn't mean what it actually says!

Still another treasure among these riches I have found is the dietary instruction as described in Leviticus 11 by our loving Father. My whole life I was taught that this was 'bondage' and 'for the Jews.' Yet, *my experience* has been radically different. Yes, on occasion I miss a few of those things left behind, but in the pressing on toward the high calling of Messiah, there has been much joy, peace and blessing. And, Scripture means what Scripture says. No tap dancing, just simple truth!

Even now, as I ponder my new found treasures of the feasts and Shabbat, another thought teases my mind.

Is it possible to have the sizzle without the steak? Or would that only be a vain imagining?

I was raised in a foreign/Latin culture for six of the first ten years of my life. I experienced the richness of Colombian life by living there. My knowledge base today, though limited by the youth of my experience, is not based on an encyclopedia of reading about the people, the culture or the food. Neither is it based on the Travel channel or some local restaurant's limited menu. Rather, I *experienced* the culture, food and people and can still these forty years later taste certain foods or crave certain fresh fruit. Why? Because I lived it!

Whatever possibly made me think I could understand Pesach or Sukkot, or my Mashiach as the Passover Lamb because I read *about* Passover or the Feast of Booths in some Bible encyclopedia? The richness of the lessons learned through *experience* the first two times my family and I celebrated these (and other) feasts added much more depth than forty years in the church including seminary and ten years in the pulpit. Pure folly to think I could understand without *experiencing* the richness. I have indeed found a treasure!

No wonder Rav Shaul (Apostle Paul) says, "Keep the feast!" and indeed, kept the feasts himself. He further enjoins us to "follow me as I follow Messiah." If we are following Shaul's example, and that of Yeshua, we will stumble right into the treasures of the Feasts of Yahweh (Feasts of the Lord), Shabbat, a Biblical diet, and other blessings.

At some point we will address Shaul more deeply, but for those who would seek truth, I recommend the Pauline Paradox series by 119 Ministries. What does Scripture *really* say? Not, 'what does your doctrine say?'

I might also recommend the rest of the RT series. (Yes, shameless self-promotion...lol!) These are designed to help put together some other pieces of Scripture that have been hidden by doctrines of men.

Simply, pray and ask our Father to reveal Truth!! Read with an open Bible and compare what is written with what you have been taught. There are great riches in coming to the Truth.

RT: Syncretism

Originally posted on February 25, 2013.

While my dad was well educated and enjoyed academic pursuits, he would sometimes give a person a hard time for using unnecessarily large words. "Two dollar words" he called them. In his wisdom, he understood that often 'less is more.'

Today is not such a day. Today, we pull out a 'two dollar word' because nothing else will precisely fit.

I give you,

> **syn·cre·tism** : [sing-kri-tiz-uh m, sin-] *noun*
> 1. the attempted reconciliation or union of different or opposing principles, practices, or parties, as in philosophy or religion.
> 2. *Grammar.* the merging, as by historical change in a language, of two or more categories in a specified environment into one, as, in nonstandard English, the use of was with both singular and plural subjects, while in standard English was is used with singular subjects (except for you in the second person singular) and were with plural subjects.
> *Origin:*
> 1610–20; < Neo-Latin syncretismus < Greek synkrētismós union of Cretans, i.e., a united front of two opposing parties against a common foe, derivative of synkrēt (ízein) to syncretize + -ismos -ism

From childhood, those who are raised in Christendom are taught to wag their finger and 'tsk, tsk, tsk' at 'those fickle Israelites' for having the audacity to make a golden calf. In fact, they did it at the base of Mt. Sinai within view of the fire and smoke! In the previous couple months they had seen wonders in Egypt, enjoyed miraculous salvation, and been provided for with manna and quail. They had *just* been given the commandments, had clearly heard them and were in great awe of their Elohim (God). How could they be so fickle?

If we go back and look at the text carefully we will find something very interesting!

In spite of violating clear commands, they thought they were doing rightly! I kid you not. This wasn't a blatant rebellion in their eyes. They were just doing what they thought best... and in that is the problem. Man's wisdom. But, I am getting ahead of myself.

After Moshe had been on the mountain for some time, nearly forty days if I recall, the sons of Israel began to get antsy. With their trust in him, rather than their Deliverer, they decided to take matters into their own hands. Notice that it is the preachers, er, Levites that are complicit in appeasing the people.

Aharon leads the charge by collecting an offering of gold and fashions the molten calf. He then declares, "This is your elohim (supreme godhead!) who brought you up from the land of Egypt."

The audacity! But it gets worse! He went on to 'build an altar before it' and proclaim, "tomorrow is a feast to Yahweh!" Seriously, he actually calls it by the name of the eternally self-existing El! "Yahweh."

I think we wrongly believe that Aharon made some wild radical departure from the faith of his fathers and wandered into pagan idolatry, but the text reveals something far more sinister.

Aharon led the people in **syncretism**.

Let's go back and reread the first part of our definition and absorb the gravity of what is happening. **Syncretism** is *"the attempted reconciliation or union of different or opposing principles, practices, or parties, as in philosophy or religion."*

Aharon is overseeing the mixing of truth and falsehood. It is carefully crafted to have elements of truth mixed with some error in order to appease the people and maintain position of power and authority, the Commandments be damned.

Notice that everything about the whole event is in keeping with the Word of Yahweh except the minor detail of a graven image. The god they are worshipping is named Yahweh. They build an altar to it and offer "burnt offerings and peace offerings." They have a feast.

Syncretism is the mixing of truth and falsehood. Yahweh calls this an abomination!

Simply, Yahweh is very precise throughout His Word to tell us exactly how He wants to be worshipped. Adding to or taking away from His Word, particularly when mixing pagan practices, is utterly detestable in His sight. It is a vile and detestable thing to the living Elohim.

The 'golden calf incident' is not alone in Scripture as an example of detestable syncretism. In fact, both the House of Israel and the house of Judah went on to perfect this model.

While the Bible is full of examples of worship on the high places and in the groves, etc., there are a number of very specific examples of **syncretism**.

In I Kings 12: 25-33 we see Jeroboam specifically altering the time and place of worship and feasts *for no other reason than to protect his own power base* and perpetuate the division wrought in the kingdom. Just a few generations later, Elijah had a showdown with the very descendants of this syncretistic mix of the things of Yahweh and paganism. Later, the woman at the well relates to Yeshua this enduring division in form or practice of worship that was so detestable to Yahweh that was still going on in Samaria.

Judah was not exempt. You remember the serpent that was lifted up in the wilderness (Num. 21:9)? Apparently, so did Judah, because they kept the icon in the Temple and burned incense to it for nearly 1000 years before Hezekiah broke it to pieces (2 Ki 18:1). What was it doing in the Temple?? When had Yahweh ever said anything about keeping it and making it into an icon of worship? **Syncretism.** Melding false pagan practices with the true worship of the living Elohim.

Ezekiel, in chapter 8,relates multiple "abominations" in a single chapter. Sun god worship within the temple courts, idol worship within the elder's homes, worship of Tammuz by the women, etc... **Syncretism.** Remember, they are doing this within the temple, between the altar and the courts. This is a melding of pagan practices and the ways of the Eternal El.

It is interesting to note in our definition that the origin of the word can be chased back to the Greek 'synkretismos' meaning, union of Cretans. The idea pictured is uniting two opposing parties against a common foe.

Brilliant, and an exact image of how we find so much syncretism within the religion known as Christianity.

A cursory study of 'church history' will reveal that the Roman Catholic Church, much like Jeroboam, is the result of using the powerful elixir of syncretism to appease pagans and Christians while garnering wealth and authority and the subjugation of all things "Jewish." Now, those who know history well will view this as overly simplistic since the formation of the RCC happened well after Jerusalem was destroyed, but follow me here.

Even the Apostle Paul was in a continuous running battle with Greek Gnostics who were already infiltrating the sect called The Way to co-opt it for their own twisted purposes. Within a century of Yeshua's death the race was on in earnest to separate The Way from any vestige of Hebrew root while filling the void with altered pagan customs. By the time of Constantine, the Roman bishops were renaming ancient pagan holidays and 'christianizing them' (the definition of **syncretism!**) to suit their own lusts for wealth, control and power.

Don't believe me? Go do a web search for pagan ties between Easter and the fertility goddess Ostare, with variants including:

Ostara, Ostern, Eostra, Eostre, Eostur, Eastra, Eastur, Austron and Ausos. Any of those are easily traced back into Babylonian pagan fertility rites complete with bunnies, dyed eggs, ham, etc...

Okay, so that wasn't so fun. Maybe just an anomaly. Try a similar search for pagan ties between Christmas and Saturnalia. Watch out because this ancient festival that predates Yeshua by 500+ years includes such trappings as evergreens, late December observance, gifts, a tree, mistletoe, etc...

As believers in Jesus, we like to think we have it all together. It comes as a shock to find that in fact there is MUCH syncretism within our own doctrines and traditions. Still, if we worship an Elohim who is unchanging, the same yesterday, today and forever, and His Word is Truth, then, we should be anxious to root out any and all falsehood in our worship, particularly those parts that have clear pagan origins which are an abomination as described in Deuteronomy 12:29-32.

Syncretism is something we must abhor as much as our Creator does. It is a vile, detestable affront to Yahweh's specified manner of worship.

Here are a couple well researched and riveting videos with a wealth of information supporting the charge that the church is steeped in **syncretism.**
119ministries.com/teachings/video-teachings/detail/sunburned-part-1/
119ministries.com/teachings/video-teachings/detail/sunburned-part-2/

We live in incredible times, prophetically! Yahweh is preparing to judge the earth and judgment always begins at the house of the Lord. Revelation 18 has a stern warning against drinking from the fount of syncretism.

I pray that you will be shocked awake and run, not walk, away from falsehood and toward the true worship of the Living Elohim.

RT: Signs

Originally posted on March 2, 2013.

Signs, signs, everywhere a sign.

As with my other RT posts, proceed with caution.

Scripture articulates several particular signs that point to very specific promises. Some we heed, and to our peril, some we not only ignore, but we intentionally spray paint over in an effort to hide the signs for those who come behind...

Can you imagine hiking in the mountains and encountering a sign warning of snakes or bears that someone who went before you painted over or in some other way defaced or obscured so that you would not see it?? Not a pleasant picture. Even worse is seeing the sign and having someone you trust standing there telling you the sign doesn't really mean what it says.

Christendom has several such signs that have been painted over or otherwise defaced, and there are innumerable people you and I trust standing there telling us the sign doesn't mean what it says. We will only look at one altered sign in this post. (And tell you who altered it and stands next to it pointing the other way.)

To set the stage, let's be reminded of some of the **signs** we love and hold dear. These we can use for comparison to the sign that has been defaced.

Perhaps the most often referred to **sign** is the 'bow.' (Gen. 9)
Genesis 9:8-17
Then God spoke to Noah and to his sons with him, saying, "Now behold, I Myself do establish My covenant with you, and with your descendants after you; ··· all flesh shall <u>never again</u> be cut off by the water of the flood . . . This is the **sign** of the covenant . . . I set My bow in the cloud, and it shall be for a **sign** of a covenant between Me and the earth . . . When the bow is in the

cloud, then I will look upon it, to remember the everlasting covenant between God and every living creature of all flesh that is on the earth." And God said to Noah, "This is the **sign** of the covenant ..."

There are three elements here that are worthy of note. 'Covenant,' 'sign' and 'forever' (never again or everlasting...).

This is a promise we 'hang our hat on!' God is a God of covenant, an Elohim of promise. He says, (paraphrasing) "I will ..., forever!" We absolutely believe in this as an unchanging and unchangeable promise. (Remember, Yahweh does NOT change. A promise is a promise. Particularly when stated in these covenantal terms.)

How about another one? The Abrahamic Covenant.

Genesis 17:1-11
Now when Abram was ninety-nine years old, the Lord appeared to Abram and said to him, "I am, God Almighty; walk before Me, and be blameless. I will establish My covenant between Me and you, and I will multiply you exceedingly." Abram fell on his face, and God talked with him, saying, "As for Me, behold, My covenant is with you, and you will be the father of a multitude of nations. No longer shall your name be called Abram, but your name shall be Abraham; for I have made you the father of a multitude of nations. I will make you exceedingly fruitful, and I will make nations of you, and kings will come forth from you. I will establish My covenant between Me and you and your descendants after you throughout their generations for an everlasting covenant, to be God to you and to your descendants after you. I will give to you and to your descendants after you, the land of your sojournings, all the land of Canaan, for an everlasting possession; and I will be their God . . . And you shall be circumcised in the flesh of your foreskin, and it shall be the **sign** of the covenant between Me and you."

Here we have the same 'formula.' Covenant-**sign**-forever.

Both of the preceding covenants and their 'everlasting' nature are a settled matter in all of 'Christian history.' Nobody in their right mind would argue that the earth can again be destroyed by a flood. In the same vein, only an avowed anti-Semite would argue that the covenant of the land and the blessing upon Abraham are debatable.

The Davidic Covenant is another 'forever covenant' though the sign is a little less obvious, at least for now. Yahweh made a promise to David that He, the Everlasting One, would establish David's throne forever. Yeshua, the rightful heir, is King and will again walk in Jerusalem as King. Forever.

Ezekiel confirms this in 37:24-28. He quotes Yahweh saying,

Ezekiel 37:24-28
"My servant David will be king over them, and they will all have one shepherd; and they will walk in My ordinances and keep My statutes and observe them. hey will live on the land that I gave to Jacob My servant, in which your fathers lived; and they will live on it, they, and their sons and their sons' sons, <u>forever</u>; and David My servant will be their prince <u>forever</u>. I will make a covenant of peace with them; it will be an <u>everlasting covenant</u> with them. And I will place them and multiply them, and will set My sanctuary in their midst <u>forever</u>. My dwelling place also will be with them; and I will be their God, and they will be My people. And the nations will know that I am the Lord who sanctifies Israel, when My sanctuary is in their midst <u>forever</u>.

Notice, this is a fulfillment of an everlasting covenant that involves the land and Yeshua ben David (Jesus Son of David), as the fulfilling **sign**, as well as another interesting element... and here is where the whole 'sign-covenant-forever' signpost gets blurred if we listen to Christian theologians.

Don't listen to me. Let's just look at Scripture. No doctrines of men. Just the everlasting Word.

Our previous passage from Ezekiel said,
> My servant David will be king over them, and they will all have one shepherd; and **they will walk in My ordinances and keep My statutes and observe them**.

Hmmm...

"Ethel, did that boy just say we have to keep the Commandments?"

"Mmmm. No, I think that's what he thinks that verse says."

Okay, I guess we need more Scripture... "So the sons of Israel shall observe the Sabbath, to celebrate the Sabbath throughout their generations as a <u>perpetual covenant</u>.' It is a **sign** between Me and the sons of Israel <u>forever</u>;..."

Oh, look. 'Covenant-**Sign**-Forever.' In case you think I made that up, look at Exodus 31:12-17. The context is even more explicit.

Bet your pastor didn't see that **sign**.

Frankly, I didn't either. For years! (Read RT: Antisemitism for a full confession! Of course, now you need 'Grafting' and 'Olam!' as well.)

Maybe here is a good place to consider two important verses, the first prophetic and the second instructive:
> **Jeremiah 16:19**
> Our fathers have inherited nothing but falsehood, futility and things of no profit." (Jer. 16:14-21 for context)

And...
> **Jeremiah 31:35**
> Thus says Yahweh, Who gives the sun for light by day and the fixed order of the moon and the stars for light by night, Who stirs up the sea so that its waves roar; Yahweh Sabaoth is His name: "If this fixed order departs from before Me," declares Yahweh, "Then the

offspring of Israel also will cease from being a nation before Me forever." (See Jer. 31:31-37)

[Before quoting something about the 'New Covenant' you might want to read the previous context and see WHO the covenant is with and WHAT will be written on their hearts... Check the Hebrew for absolute clarity!]

Earlier, you may have thought, "Yeah, but this Sabbath thing, that's for the sons of Israel. That's what the verse says."

Yep, you would be right. But so is the New Covenant. "House of Israel, House of Judah" ring a bell? See Hebrews 8:8 then re-read RT: Grafting.

Or, maybe I can challenge tradition another way: The Ezekiel passage above says, "My servant David will be king over them, and they will all have one shepherd; and they will walk in My ordinances and keep My statutes and observe them. ²⁵ They will live on the land that I gave to Jacob My servant, in which your fathers lived; and they will live on it, they, and their sons and their sons' sons, <u>forever</u>; and David My servant will be their prince <u>forever</u>."

If the Good Shepherd, the Servant David referenced here who will be king over them <u>forever</u>, is your King, then you will be in this kingdom that is obedient to Yahweh's statutes and ordinances. Yeshua ben David will not be king over any other kingdom if He is the King of this one <u>forever</u>.

Yeshua said, "Do not think that I came to abolish the Law or the Prophets; **I did not come to abolish** but to fulfill. For truly I say to you, until heaven and earth pass away, not the smallest letter or stroke shall pass from the Law until all is accomplished. Whoever then annuls one of the least of these commandments, and teaches others *to do* the same, shall be called least in the kingdom of heaven; but whoever keeps and teaches *them*, he shall be called great in the kingdom of heaven."

Simply, He NEVER changed the day of rest from Sabbath to SUNday. Neither did any of the Apostles or authors of Scripture.

In fact, the Roman Catholic Church proudly proclaims that THEY changed the sign post!

Let me leave you with a verse and a couple links for further research.

This is what the Lord says:
Jeremiah 6:16
Stand at the crossroads and look; ask for the ancient paths, ask where the good way is, and walk in it, and you will find rest for your souls. But you said, 'We will not walk in it.' (Jeremiah 6:16, see the rest in context, especially v. 19)

[Yeshua's yoke is ease and His burden light... Walking in Torah is where you will find rest, liberty and peace!]

Want to come out refined as pure gold? Walk in HIS ways and paths.
"But He knows the way I take;
When He has tried me, I shall come forth as gold.
"My foot has held fast to **His path**; I have kept **His way** and not turned aside. (Job 23:10-11)

And the links..

The First day of the Week
http://q.b5z.net/i/u/10105283/f/The_First_Day_and_th e_Seventh_Day_-_A_Sabbath_Study.pdf

(The quotes from the Roman Catholic Church at the end of this article are particularly instructive. They identify WHO obliterated this sign post.)

May Yahweh guide and bless you as you seek truth.

RT: Righteousness

Originally posted on April 3, 2013.

Last year was the first year my family and I celebrated Passover. It was a huge blessing, but I really didn't 'get' the whole Days of Unleavened Bread 'thing' so we let it slip by...

How much we missed!!

As we approached Pesach this year I determined to learn more about the related feast, Days of Unleavened Bread. I have learned so, so much!!

Today, my understanding of righteousness from a Scriptural perspective took a major leap forward!!

As my previous post hints, Unleavened, as all the Feasts of Yahweh, is an illustration. This particular feast teaches of the leavening/"yeasty" effect of sin in our lives. Rav Shaul says, "... a little leaven leavens the whole lump..." If we are to learn from the Feast, then, as we remove all *physical* leaven from the house, we should really be pondering the *spiritual* leaven in our lives. In that vein, I have been really seeking understanding on 'righteousness.'

That led me today to an interesting passage of Scripture: 2 Samuel 22:21-25

2 Samuel 22:21-25
Yahweh **has rewarded me according to my righteousness**;
According to the cleanness of my hands He has recompensed me.
For I have kept the ways of Yahweh, and have not acted wickedly against my God.
For all His ordinances *were* before me, and *as for* His statutes, I did not depart from them.
I was also blameless toward Him, And I kept myself from my iniquity.
Therefore Yahweh **has recompensed me according to**

my righteousness,
According to my cleanness before His eyes.

I don't know about you, but that set off an alarm. Raised in the church, I had always been taught, directly or indirectly that 'my righteousness' is of no value. Generally, the phrase from Isaiah 64:6 comes to mind: "...*all our righteous deeds are like a filthy garment*...."

So, today I read the larger context of the Isaiah passage and a different picture comes into view. Thus, the error of proof-texting to support false teachings is again exposed! But, I digress...

In the larger context it becomes clear that the ones Yahweh is dressing down are NOT doing things HIS way. They are pursuing their own agenda. Verses 6 & 7 indicate they are involved in the unclean, they do not know His name and He has delivered them into the powers of their iniquities which leads to blindness.

Now, as I was raised, there really were only two kinds of righteousness taught: 1) the righteousness of Christ and 2) all other righteousness that is as filthy rags. Comparing the two passages above, however, reveals something.

It would seem there are actually **three types of righteousness** in view.
- The righteousness of Yeshua/Christ/Messiah
- My righteousness according to HIS ways
- My righteousness according to MY ways...

Let's test this with a few verses.

Understand up front, I can do NOTHING that merits salvation. Yeshua is the only acceptable atoning sacrifice before Yahweh. So, *we are not talking about salvation*. We are talking about the walk of righteousness and our relationship to it.

Deuteronomy 6:24-25 says:
Deuteronomy 6:24-25

So the Lord commanded us to observe all these statutes, to fear the Lord our God for our good always and for our survival, as *it is* today. **It will be righteousness for us** if we are careful to observe all this commandment before the Lord our God, just as He commanded us.

This would seem to be at least one of the verses David is pondering when he says, *"Yahweh has rewarded me according to **my righteousness**; According to the cleanness of my hands He has recompensed me. ²²"For I have **kept the ways of Yahweh**,..."*

Isaiah 58 seems to speak a similar message. The people are complaining to Yahweh because they fast, but He does not hear. He points out that they are not doing what He desires, keeping His commands, etc. He says in verse 8, "[if you will do that] *Then your light will break out like the dawn, and your recovery will speedily spring forth; and **your righteousness** will go before you; the glory of the LORD will be your rear guard...*"

Hmmm...

There are numerous other verses that advance this line of thought. For brevity sake, consider these references:
"own righteousness" Ez. 14:14;
"practice righteousness and live" Ez. 18:5, 9, 17, 19, 21, 24, and 27
"cleanse ourselves from all defilement of flesh and spirit" 2 Cor. 6:14-7:1
"...achieve the righteousness of God... [by being] an effectual doer..." James, in 1:20-25, contrasts sin (anger, wickedness, etc) with the 'perfect Law of Liberty.'

Here's the point, once we are saved by the atoning sacrifice of Yeshua, we are called to walk in the 'paths of righteousness for His name's sake.' That path of righteousness is not an ethereal path we get to define as some moral code based on the traditions of men or doctrinal statements. ("Don't drink, smoke or chew, or go out with girls who do.")

No, Abba gives a very clear definition of what righteousness looks like and how we are to 'walk' in it.

Problems begin when teachers, using man-made doctrines create little codes that *they deem* to be the path of sanctification. Then, they declare to be seeking self-righteousness anyone who actually seeks to do all of the Creator's Commandments that "**will be righteousness for us.**"

The question then that we must ask ourselves is: Am I pursuing righteousness according to the doctrines of men, or according to the revealed righteousness of God? Yahweh clearly defines for us what righteousness looks like. It looks like Yeshua, the Living Word revealing Torah, the written Word. Yeshua was sinless according to Torah and we are called to 'walk as He walked.'

Walking according to a doctrinal statement or theological statement that runs counter to Torah is self-righteousness. It is the righteousness of men.

Just as we have been challenged by the task of removing the physical leaven from our house, we have been challenged by where we find some of the spiritual leaven... many traditions, common in the church, are leaven that need to be purged.

It is not easy, but I challenge you to honestly evaluate every part of how you worship and why you do it! Is it prescribed by Scripture, or tradition? Find the verses and prove it!

You may be very surprised that the ancient paths have never changed, contrary to most church doctrines.

Jeremiah the prophet, in chapter 6 says,

> **Jeremiah 6:16-19**
> Thus says the Lord, "Stand by the ways and see and **ask for the ancient paths**, where the good way is, **and walk in it**; and **you will find rest for your souls**. But they said, 'We will not walk *in it*.' And I set watchmen over you, *saying*, 'Listen to the sound of the trumpet!' But they said, 'We will not listen.' "Therefore hear, O

nations, and know, O congregation, what is among them. Hear, O earth: behold, **I am bringing disaster on this people,** the fruit of their plans, **because they have not listened to My words,** and **as for My law (Torah), they have rejected it** also."

I pray you are challenged to dig in and study. You will find rest for your souls. Indeed HIS burden is light.

RT: Torah

Originally posted on May 21, 2013.

Having served in the military, I know just how crazy and dangerous is the situation when someone throws a hand grenade into a crowded room. The reactions are varied, but all extreme. One may instantly choose to fall on the grenade, while most dive to the floor or hit the exits as aggressively as possible. All react on pure instinct. There is NO time to think. Only, REACT!

The word 'Torah' is a verbal hand grenade that engenders a near identical response.

I want to ask you to take a deep breath and relax. If this is a new or troubling term to you, do not worry. This book will not explode or burst into flame. You have time to think and process.

Generally speaking, Christendom defines 'Torah' as LAW... and "LAW is baaaad."

Well, for this segment, we are not going to consider or even care what the Church thinks... Let's see what Scripture says.

If Scripture is the inerrant, inspired Word of the Living God, then surely we can trust what it says as the measure of Truth! How does the everlasting Word define 'Torah?'
- The Torah is perfect: Psalm 19:7, James 1:25
- The Torah is life and peace: Proverbs 3:1-2; Proverbs 6:23; Revelation 22:14; Psalm 119:165
- The Torah is the way: Exodus 18:20; Psalm 119:1; Proverbs 6:23; Isaiah 2:3; Malachi 2:8
- The Torah is truth: Malachi 2:6
- The Torah is light: Proverbs 6:23; Isaiah 2:3-5; 8:20; 51:4

Remember, Yeshua is the Living Word, the Word made flesh, the light of the world, the Way, the Truth, the Life.

- The Torah defines how to love Yahweh: Joshua 22:5; Psalm 119:34
- The Torah defines Yahweh's will: Psalm 40:8
- The Torah defines sin: Jeremiah 44:23; Daniel 9:11; 1 John 3:4; Romans 7:7

Starting to get the picture? This is ONLY using verses where the word 'torah' appears in the Hebrew with a couple select NT verses. There are hundreds, HUNDREDS of similar verses using synonyms for the word 'torah.' Please take the time to read Psalm 119 and highlight every synonym referring to 'Torah.' ... Judgments, statutes, commands, ways, testimonies, precepts, ordinances, wonders, etc.

So why is this so important? Generally speaking, the Church teaches that 'the Law kills.' Generally speaking, they teach that 'the Law has been abolished.'

And, generally speaking, they are absolutely wrong.

The Torah's own testimony of itself is that it is life, peace, liberty, the way, truth, honey, wine, etc. In short, it blesses those who are obedient to it and it curses those who are not.

Please understand, I am NOT saying that there is not life and peace in Messiah Yeshua. He absolutely IS Life and Peace. Remember, He said, "I did NOT come to abolish the Law, but to fulfill... not one jot or title will pass from the Law until heaven and earth pass away..."

What I am saying is that Torah is what Yeshua came to redeem us to. He came to restore us to the covenant. (See the reNewed Covenant in Jeremiah 31:31-34 and notice that what is to be written on our hearts is Torah.... v. 33) We are enabled, by the Spirit, to walk obediently as He walked. In Torah we find life and peace.

Psalm 19:7-14 says,
Psalm 19:7-14

The Torah of Yahweh is perfect, converting the soul: the testimony of Yahweh is sure, making wise the simple.

The statutes of Yahweh are right, rejoicing the heart: the commandment of Yahweh is pure, enlightening the eyes.

The fear of Yahweh is clean, enduring forever: the judgments of Yahweh are true and righteous altogether.

More to be desired are they than gold, yea, than much fine gold: sweeter also than honey and the honeycomb.

Moreover by them is thy servant warned: and **in keeping of them there is great reward.**

Who can understand his errors? Cleanse thou me from secret faults.

Keep back thy servant also from presumptuous sins; let them not have dominion over me: then shall I be upright, and I shall be innocent from the great transgression.

Let the words of my mouth, and the meditation of my heart, be acceptable in thy sight, O Yahweh, my strength, and my redeemer.

Once we overcome the false paradigm that Torah is "baaaad" and begin to understand that over and over in Scripture we are commanded to follow and that blessings come from obedience to Torah, God's Instructions, THEN we can begin to fully understand Messiah, Yahweh and Scripture. Not before. Any understanding of Scripture that does away with Torah completely violates and warps the whole book and all we read in it.

If this has challenged you and you want to study further, here are a few links for more information:
- Teshuva Ministries: http://teshuvaministries.net/getting-started/
- https://natsab.wordpress.com/resources/

I pray this has been a blessing to you and pray you will study this out. Shalom!

3 CONSIDERING THE SABBATH

Possibly the single most challenging hurdle we overcame as my family began to seek to walk as our Messiah walked was switching from Sunday to Sabbath worship. Truly, in Christendom, even if we do not keep Sunday observance holy, or set apart, we do consider the tradition a sacred institution.

I had been a pastor for 10 years at the point that God began to seriously challenge my practice. Breaking the tradition that had been ingrained in me caused much personal angst, a battle I fought by continually returning to the Word of God and reading what it said without the filters of men.

Following are several posts dealing with this very topic from various angles. Some of the approaches are very bold. Please understand, dear reader, that I am not trying to be abrasive or offensive, but I do want to shock us into reality. Let us take off the filters of tradition and doctrine and simply see what the everlasting and unchanging Word of our King says.

Christians, please help me understand...

Originally posted on January 27, 2014.

I have four boys, most of whom are teenagers. We do not have a communication problem, so I can tell them what to do and they understand perfectly well.

If I tell them clearly, once or twice, to do something, should I have a reasonable expectation that they will do it? What if I clearly give them the same instructions five times?

Suppose I give my sons the *exact same instructions* eight or even NINE times and I NEVER tell them anything different? Do I have a reasonable expectation that I have been very clear? If they continue to disobey me on the matter, do I have a right to discipline them? Can they plead ignorance? What if the babysitter tells them otherwise? Whose instructions take priority, mine or the sitter? Does the babysitter have authority to overturn my instructions?

See? This is the dilemma I am in, now. I was that wayward teen who heard my Father say something nine times, but I ignored it because the babysitter said it was okay. Now, I am looking back and realizing I was/am without excuse. His instructions were very clearly given and never changed. Was my disobedience sin?

Later, I was the babysitter who told those in my care that they could just ignore what their Father had said. I supported what I said with some fancy logic, but had no real evidence that their Father had ever changed His instructions.

So what exactly am I getting at? (And, what do I want you to help me understand?)

Our Father in heaven gives us a commandment NINE times, and we ignore it. Nowhere in Scripture does He ever change His mind. Nowhere is the command ever altered. In fact, prophecy actually tells us a couple times that the command stands in the future, yet we ignore it, preferring the logical gymnastics of our pastors and the traditions we have been handed.

With Scripture being so clear, will we be able to plead ignorance?

Here is the commandment... all NINE times:

Exodus 20:9-11
Remember the Sabbath day, to keep it holy. Six days you shall labor and do all your work, but **the seventh day is a Sabbath of the Lord your God**; in it you shall not do any work, you or your son or your daughter, your male or your female servant or your cattle or your sojourner who stays with you. For in six days the Lord made the heavens and the earth, the sea and all that is in them, and rested on **the seventh day**; therefore the Lord blessed the Sabbath day and made it holy.

Exodus 16:25-30
Moses said, "Eat it today, for today is a Sabbath to the Lord; today you will not find it in the field. Six days you shall gather it, but on **the seventh day, the Sabbath**, there will be none." It came about on the seventh day that some of the people went out to gather, but they found none. Then the Lord said to Moses, "How long do you refuse to keep My commandments and My instructions? See, the Lord has given you the Sabbath; therefore He gives you bread for two days on the sixth day. Remain every man in his place; let no man go out of his place on **the seventh day**." So the people rested on the seventh day.

Exodus 23:12
Six days you are to do your work, but **on the seventh day you shall cease from labor** so that your ox and your donkey may rest, and the son of your female slave, as well as your stranger, may refresh themselves.

Exodus 31:12-17

The Lord spoke to Moses, saying, "But as for you, speak to the sons of Israel, saying, 'You shall surely observe My Sabbaths; for this is a sign between Me and you throughout your generations, that you may know that I am the Lord who sanctifies you. Therefore you are to observe the Sabbath, for it is holy to you. Everyone who profanes it shall surely be put to death; for whoever does any work on it, that person shall be cut off from among his people. For six days work may be done, but **on the seventh day there is a Sabbath of complete rest**, holy to the Lord; whoever does any work on the Sabbath day shall surely be put to death. So the sons of Israel shall observe the Sabbath, to celebrate the Sabbath throughout their generations as a perpetual covenant.' It is a sign between Me and the sons of Israel forever; for in six days the Lord made heaven and earth, but **on the seventh day He ceased from labor**, and was refreshed."

Exodus 34:21

You shall work six days, but on **the seventh day you shall rest**; even during plowing time and harvest you shall rest.

Exodus 35:2

For six days work may be done, but on **the seventh day** you shall have a holy Sabbath of complete rest to the Lord; whoever does any work on it shall be put to death.

Leviticus 23:2-4

"Speak to the sons of Israel and say to them, 'The Lord's appointed times which you shall proclaim as holy convocations—My appointed times are these: "For six days work may be done, but **on the seventh day** there is a Sabbath of complete rest, a holy convocation. You shall not do any work; it is a Sabbath to the Lord in all your dwellings. These are the appointed times of the

Lord, holy convocations which you shall proclaim at the times appointed for them."'"

Deuteronomy 5:12-15
Observe the Sabbath day to keep it holy, as the Lord your God commanded you. Six days you shall labor and do all your work, but **the seventh day is a Sabbath of the Lord** your God; in it you shall not do any work, you or your son or your daughter or your male servant or your female servant or your ox or your donkey or any of your cattle or your sojourner who stays with you, so that your male servant and your female servant may rest as well as you. You shall remember that you were a slave in the land of Egypt, and the Lord your God brought you out of there by a mighty hand and by an outstretched arm; therefore the Lord your God commanded you to observe the Sabbath day.

Genesis 1:31-2:3
God saw all that He had made, and behold, it was very good. And there was evening and there was morning, the sixth day. Thus the heavens and the earth were completed, and all their hosts. By the seventh day God completed His work which He had done, and **He rested on the seventh day** from all His work which He had done. Then **God blessed the seventh day and sanctified it**, because in it He rested from all His work which God had created and made.

Now, where is this ever changed? Our Father gave us this commandment NINE times. It may be the clearest and most attested instruction in all of Scripture. Certainly, we see Yeshua keeping the Shabbat. Read Acts. Paul always kept the Shabbat. In fact, there is not a single instance in all of Scripture of the Sabbath being changed, annulled, abrogated, altered, abolished, done away with, or any other euphemistic denial of the command.

Isaiah 66:23 tells us the Sabbath will be kept after the earth is judged by fire (66:16-17)!!

So, here is what I need help understanding: By what leap of logic do we trust the words of pastors over the Word of our Father? Will we not be held accountable for ignoring His commands and following the counter-instructions of others?

Show me! I just can't find any Scripture that prophesies or commands a change. I find no support in Scripture for a change of days. Zero. None. Nil. Zilch. Nada!

Can God 'unsanctify' the 'sanctified?'

Originally posted on January 31, 2015.

Yesterday evening I was test driving my new "toy," a new Bible translation, from Messianic Jewish Family Bible (MJFB). I was selecting and reading random texts and considering the phrasing to gain insight into the minds of the translators when I thought to look at Genesis 2:2-3. The MJFB's Tree of Life Version renders the verses,

Genesis 2:2-3
God completed – on the seventh day – His work that He made, and He ceased – on the seventh day – from all His work that He made. Then God blessed the seventh day and sanctified it, for on it He ceased from all His work that God created for the purpose of preparing.

The phrase – "and sanctified it" – leapt off the page. Immediately a question popped into my head, "Can God 'unsanctify' something He has already 'sanctified?'

I stared at the ceiling pondering and Jeremiah, my then 15 year old second born asked what I was thinking. (They know the look when wheels are turning...)

"Can God 'unsanctify' something He has already sanctified?," I mused. "By that I mean, can He profane, or make common, something that *He* has set apart as holy?"

Almost immediately Jeremiah retorted, "No, because that would make Him a liar."

"How so?" I pressed.

"Because, He would have to go back on His Word."

"Exactly." I was proud. He is learning. We midrashed it a bit leading to more thoughts.

This morning the thoughts again crossed my mind and I pondered Numbers 15:32-36 (TLV)

Numbers 15:32-36
While Bnei-Ysrael were in the wilderness, they found a man gathering wood on the Shabbat. Those who found him gathering wood brought him to Moses, Aaron and the entire assembly. They kept him under arrest, not being clear what was to be done to him. Adonai said to Moses, "The man has to die; the whole assembly is to stone him with stones outside the camp." So the whole assembly took him outside the camp. They stoned him with stones. He died just as Adonai commanded Moses.

IF, big 'if,' God changed the day to the first/eighth day, as Christendom teaches, would God not need to apologize to this poor soul for putting him to death for breaking a standard that wasn't really permanent? Seriously.

I remember when my family was just making this transition to Shabbat and I had a protracted debate with an area pastor. I asserted that God did not and indeed cannot change the day. To do so would be to deny Himself. The pastor countered that God can do anything He wants and can change the rules anytime He wants.

I was aghast!

A God that can 'willy-nilly' change the rules at any time can't be trusted and is nothing more than a schizophrenic psycho. Imagine this nightmare: EVERY promise in Scripture is subject to change!

If His Word reveals His character and His Word is unchanging, then His character is unchanging and therefore altogether trustworthy.

I would ask again, Can God 'unsanctify' that which He has 'sanctified?' Can He 'profane' that which He has called 'holy?' Can He make 'common' that which He has called 'set-apart?'

Absolutely NOT!

Malachi 3:6

For I, the Lord, do not change; therefore you, O sons of Jacob, are not consumed.

Marinate.

"all flesh".... (Does that include errant theologians?)

Originally posted on June 2, 2014.

Recently, while reading a post over on another blog, a paragraph jumped out at me with its particular focus on the phrase "all flesh," taken from Isaiah 66:23.

The paragraph that grabbed my attention:
> Christians teach that the Jewish Shabbat has been abolished. But a Messianic understands that this is a lie, that Shabbat is meant for "all flesh" and is the time that you can "know" G-d. And, as a communal day, the only way we communal beings can really "delight" in Shabbat is by breaking off from the Christian sphere of influence and joining a community that worships on Shabbat.

And, that comes from Isaiah 66:23,

Isaiah 66:22-23
> For as the **new heavens and the new earth**, which I will make, shall remain before me, saith the Lord, so shall your seed and your name remain. And it shall come to pass, that from one new moon to another, and from one Sabbath to another, shall **all flesh** come to worship before me, saith the Lord.

Please explain to me again how it is that the Sabbath, instituted in the Garden of Eden by our unchanging God and prophesied by same Self-Existing One to exist for ALL FLESH in the future, has been 'done away with' or 'replaced.'

Frankly, there is no case or any logic that surmounts the simple Scriptures. NINE times we are explicitly told that the Sabbath is the seventh day. Nowhere EVER is a change prophesied or commanded. In fact, precisely the opposite is the case. See Isaiah 56, especially verses 6-7!!

That blog has it right. "Christians teach(ing) that the Jewish Shabbat has been abolished....is a lie". . . . The yet future 'all flesh' prophesy proves this!

Tradition? or Truth?

'First day of the week'... Acts 20:7

Originally posted on January 30, 2014.

Earlier I wrote concerning the nine times we are commanded, in one form or another, to 'remember the Sabbath.' Christendom's defense for Sunday worship varies, however, the primary text is usually Acts 20:7 and the phrase, 'on the first day of the week.'

Acts 20:7
On the first day of the week, when we were gathered together to break bread, Paul began talking to them, intending to leave the next day, and he prolonged his message until midnight.

There are no places in Scripture that directly say anything whatsoever about Sunday worship or a change of the day from Sabbath to Sunday. Zero. None. Nada.

This verse is as close as we get and it has numerous challenges to surmount before even being regarded as potential evidence. Let's consider multiple reasons why this verse cannot be used as a foundation for challenging established Scripture.

1. In order to demonstrate the argument that this verse and others have to overcome, let's begin with a brief comparison of two passages. Genesis 9:12-17 and Exodus 31:12-17 (selections).

Genesis 9:12-17
God said, "This is the **sign of the covenant** which I am making between Me and you and every living creature that is with you, for **all successive generations**; I set My bow in the cloud, and it shall be for **a sign** of **a covenant** between Me and the earth. . . . When the bow is in the cloud, then I will look upon it, to remember the **everlasting covenant** between God and every living creature of all flesh that is on the earth." And God said to Noah, "This is the **sign of the covenant** which I have

established between Me and all flesh that is on the earth."

Exodus 31:12-17
The Lord spoke to Moses, saying, "But as for you, speak to the sons of Israel, saying, 'You shall surely observe My Sabbaths; for this is **a sign** between Me and you **throughout your generations**, <u>that you may know that I am the Lord who sanctifies you.</u> . . . So the sons of Israel shall observe the Sabbath, to celebrate the Sabbath **throughout their generations** as a **perpetual covenant.'** It is **a sign** between Me and the sons of Israel **forever**; for in six days the Lord made heaven and earth, but on the seventh day He ceased from labor, and was refreshed."

Notice in both of these that Yahweh establishes an 'everlasting/perpetual covenant' 'throughout/all successive generations' with a 'sign.' When Yahweh sees the sign, He remembers the covenant. So, if we understand 'covenant,' then we understand that <u>the terms cannot change</u>. Every time we see a rainbow, we know Yahweh will <u>never</u> again flood the earth. Likewise, every time the calendar hits the seventh day, we know <u>Yahweh sanctifies us</u>. Conversely, if we can make the rainbow disappear, we can abolish the covenant. In similar manner, if we can make the calendar skip the Sabbath, then we can consider Yahweh's 'set apart' day to have changed. (I think Yahweh and Yeshua both say something to that effect elsewhere. Compare Jeremiah 31:35-37 and Matthew 5:18)

So, right from the beginning, we see that the burden of proof for a change of day (Sabbath to Sunday) is, for all practical purposes, insurmountable. Still, we'll entertain Acts 20:7.

2. There is a curious phrase in Acts 20:7 that is only used nine times in Scripture, and to my knowledge, never used in any known extrabiblical or secular text contemporary to the Gospel writers. Essentially, there is something unique about this phrase. That Greek phrase is μιᾷ τῶν σαββάτων, or,

transliterated into English, 'mia tōn sabbatōn.' (Your eyes do not deceive you, you can actually read part of that!)

The phrase, in its most literal form reads 'one of the Sabbaths,' and there are a few rare translations that actually deal with the phrase in this manner. The very old Bishops Bible (predates the Geneva and the KJV...) says,

Acts 20:7
And vpon one of the Sabboth dayes, when the disciples came together for to breake bread, Paul reasoned with the, redy to depart on the morowe, and continued the worde vnto mydnyght.

Modern translators however, translate the phrase as 'first day of the week.' Let's consider the parts of the phrase:

σάββατον, G4521, appears 68 times. Of those, 59 times, it is translated as 'Sabbath.' Curiously, the only time it is translated 'week' is nine times, seven of which are all speaking of a particular day. The other two are Acts 20:7 and I Cor. 16:2.

μία, G3391, appears 67 times as an irregular form of the much more common εἷς . Of those, 58 times it is translated 'one,' and only eight times is it translated 'first,' seven of which exactly match the abnormal uses of σάββατον. Interesting.

τῶν, of G3588 is a definite article that is generally translated as 'the,' but has dozens of potential variants making the definiteness of the article a little 'squishy.'

In toto, the phrase is definitely anomalous to the nine uses in the Greek New Testament leaving us with a challenge that is too easily squeezed into the 'Sunday/first day of the week presuppositional box.' Translator bias forces an understanding that may not be intended the way it is written.

3. Even if it does mean 'first day of the week,' there is a definite problem with the context. Nearly every instance of Paul

teaching/preaching in Acts appears to occur on Sabbaths, so much so that in Acts 13:42-44, when God-fearing proselytes (Gentiles) desire to hear more, they ask for him to speak 'the next Sabbath.'

If we understand that the common practice then, and even today, was for the Sabbath worship to end with a meal, and when a special teacher was in town then teaching may follow into the evening; and, we understand the Jewish day begins at sunset, this would still put Paul's encounter with Eutychus (Acts 20:9) as happening late Saturday evening (according to our calendar). Again, this does not connect it with Sunday.

4. Of the nine uses of μιᾷ τῶν σαββάτων/mia tōn sabbatōn, seven refer to a specific day. That day is the day wherein Messiah Yeshua was first seen in His resurrected body. It was also the Day of First Fruits, or the Feast of First Fruits. It was a day that fell between Unleavened Bread (technically Pesach) and Pentecost. Of note is the fact that the other two uses of this phrase in Scripture (Acts 20:7 and I Corinthians 16:2) occur precisely between those Feasts indicating a possible connection between those days and the use of the phrase. Even more likely is the probable connection, not just with the time frame, but more precisely, First Fruits, itself!

5. The usual Greek word for 'first' is πρῶτος/protos (as in, prototype), and the usual Greek word for 'day' is ἡμέρα/hēmera. Therefore, the generally accepted Greek phrase for 'first day' is πρῶτος ἡμέρα/protos hēmera. Interestingly, Luke, the author of Acts is not ignorant of that fact demonstrated by his use of that very phrase *in the same chapter*, 20:18! This again indicates something different about the particular use of μιᾷ τῶν σαββάτων.

6. Acts 20:7 describes this time of gathering as a time wherein they 'break bread.' Some would have us believe this is a worship service ending in communion, but the text is unclear on

the matter. The context points more to a fellowship meal just like the uses of the same Greek phrase in Acts 2:42, 46 and 20:11. All point, not to 'communion,' but to fellowship meals, which helps to confirm point #3.

7. There is not another single instance in all of Scripture that even hints at Sunday worship, nevermind a change of day! Consider that the whole book of Hebrews is dedicated to making the case that Yeshua/Jesus is the perfect atoning sacrifice and a better High Priest. No such case for a change of day exists anywhere in Scripture.

Every one of these points has more depth, but for the sake of brevity, we have enough evidence to draw some conclusions. Here is a quick recap:

- First, as point #1 makes, the 'sign-covenant-forever' formula we see in Exodus 31 makes any change, by all practical measures, impossible.
- Point #2 clearly demonstrates the very real probability that the phrase is not even translated correctly.
- Points #3 and #6 demonstrate that with a Hebraic understanding of a 'day' as beginning at sunset, the whole scene very likely took place on a Saturday evening (by our calendar).
- Point #4 explains that every instance of 'the phrase' occurs in conjunction with a particular time frame and possibly Feast day.
- Point #5 articulates a specific phrase used by Luke in the same chapter that DOES mean 'first day.'
- Point #7 reveals the dearth of evidence in Scripture for any change of day of worship from Sabbath to 'First Day.'

Conclusion: Acts 20:7 is not even close to being grounds for Sunday worship. In fact, it more likely supports Feast Observance and Sabbath keeping which would be in keeping with the preponderance of evidence throughout Scripture.

'Certain of the Sabbaths,' a special name for a significant date?

As I studied this, an alternate picture began to emerge, one I had not previously considered for this particular phrase. Therefore, I propose a theory. Is it possible that this phrase, absent from all other literature, was a particular idiomatic expression within the Messianic Jewish community that pointed to a particular day that occurred during/on the heels of Unleavened and well before Pentecost/Shavuot? Is it possible that this became an alternate name among the brethren for Feast of First Fruits? Bear with me. Let's pull a couple pieces together.

First Fruits was a Sabbath/holy convocation according to my understanding of Leviticus 23, but it was not a 'High Sabbath' like Pesach or Yom Kippur.

On three occasions in the KJV, Luke, in his letter to Theophilus, uses the word μία/mia where the translators render it 'certain,' (Luke 5:12, 17; 8:22) as in, 'a certain city,' 'a certain day,' and 'a certain day.'

Putting these two pieces together, is it possible that the early believers began to refer to First Fruits as 'a Certain Sabbath,' or 'a Certain of the Sabbaths?'

Interestingly, the oldest manuscripts do not have Mark 16:9-20 which includes the phrase 'first day of the week,' where the Greek says πρῶτος

σάββατον/prōtos sabbaton. This may indicate that if/when it was added at a later date, the idiomatic phrase was already on the verge of being lost, where just seven verses earlier Mark 16:2 uses μιᾷ τῶν σαββάτων.

As an idiomatic expression, I do not believe it in any way validated Sunday, but may have been an 'inside' name for the day of Messiah's post-resurrection appearances. Paul would not have used it in dealing with Gentiles, but he does openly and often refer to 'first fruits' and Messiah's resurrection.

If all of the 'first day of the week' mistranslations were rendered 'certain of the Sabbaths,' as a name for that particular feast/resurrection* day, then all but the I Corinthians 16:2 verses would make sense, particularly when we recognize they are written well after The Day and to an audience already familiar with the Feasts/Sabbaths.

Anyway, it is something to consider when we understand the only uses of the phrase are evidenced among Messianic Jews.

* I believe the actual resurrection occurred at sunset at the end of the weekly Sabbath, over which Messiah is/was 'Lord.' See: The Easter Fraud Chart!

If this study has challenged or blessed you, please consider sharing it.

Shalom and blessings in the wonderful name of Yeshua haMashiach Sar Shalom, the risen Prince of Peace!!

Peter G. Rambo, Sr.

Countermanding the Almighty!!

Originally posted on May 28, 2013.

Is it possible to countermand Yahweh, the Eternal God? Does man or the church have the authority to reverse His everlasting decrees?

Myriad verses would shout, 'NO!!! It cannot be done.' And, that would be correct with one simple caveat. IF/when Yahweh makes a change, He always tells the prophets first.

Let's support these two assertions before proceeding.

Malachi 3:6
For I am the Lord, I change not; therefore ye sons of Jacob are not consumed.

Amos 3:7
Surely the Lord God will do nothing, but he revealeth his secret unto his servants the prophets.

Over and over in Scripture we see that Yahweh does nothing capriciously and always is very specific in what He commands.

Bearing this foundation in mind, let's take a look at a change that supposedly happened at the resurrection of Messiah.

Six times, just in the Torah, the first five books of the Bible, Yahweh explicitly commands the seventh day as a day of rest:

Genesis 2:2-3
By the seventh day God completed His work which He had done, and He rested on the seventh day from all His work which He had done. Then God blessed the seventh day and sanctified it, because in it He rested from all His work which God had created and made.

Exodus 16:22-30
Now on the sixth day they gathered twice as much bread, two omers for each one. When all the leaders of

74

the congregation came and told Moses, then he said to them, "This is what the Lord meant: Tomorrow is a Sabbath observance, a holy Sabbath to the Lord. . . Eat it today, for today is a Sabbath to the Lord; today you will not find it in the field. Six days you shall gather it, but on the seventh day, the Sabbath, there will be none."

It came about on the seventh day that some of the people went out to gather, but they found none. Then the Lord said to Moses, "How long do you refuse to keep My commandments and My instructions? See, the Lord has given you the Sabbath; therefore He gives you bread for two days on the sixth day. Remain every man in his place; let no man go out of his place on the seventh day." So the people rested on the seventh day.

Exodus 20:8-11
Remember the Sabbath day, to keep it holy. Six days you shall labor and do all your work, but the seventh day is a Sabbath of the Lord your God; in it you shall not do any work, you or your son or your daughter, your male or your female servant or your cattle or your sojourner who stays with you. For in six days the Lord made the heavens and the earth, the sea and all that is in them, and rested on the seventh day; therefore the Lord blessed the Sabbath day and made it holy.

Exodus 31:14-17
Therefore you are to observe the Sabbath, for it is holy to you. Everyone who profanes it shall surely be put to death; for whoever does any work on it, that person shall be cut off from among his people. For six days work may be done, but on the seventh day there is a Sabbath of complete rest, holy to the Lord; whoever does any work on the Sabbath day shall surely be put to death. So the sons of Israel shall observe the Sabbath, to celebrate the Sabbath throughout their generations as a perpetual covenant. It is a sign between Me and

the sons of Israel forever; for in six days the Lord made heaven and earth, but on the seventh day He ceased from labor, and was refreshed.

Leviticus 23:1-4
The Lord spoke again to Moses, saying, "Speak to the sons of Israel and say to them, 'The Lord's appointed times which you shall proclaim as holy convocations— My appointed times are these: For six days work may be done, but on the seventh day there is a Sabbath of complete rest, a holy convocation. You shall not do any work; it is a Sabbath to the Lord in all your dwellings. These are the appointed times of the Lord, holy convocations which you shall proclaim at the times appointed for them.

(Note, too, four times in this chapter, the 'appointed times of Yahweh' are listed as 'perpetual throughout your generations' (Lev. 23:14, 21, 31, 41))

Deuteronomy 5:12-15
Observe the Sabbath day to keep it holy, as the Lord your God commanded you. Six days you shall labor and do all your work, but the seventh day is a Sabbath of the Lord your God; in it you shall not do any work, you or your son or your daughter or your male servant or your female servant or your ox or your donkey or any of your cattle or your sojourner who stays with you, so that your male servant and your female servant may rest as well as you. You shall remember that you were a slave in the land of Egypt, and the Lord your God brought you out of there by a mighty hand and by an outstretched arm; therefore the Lord your God commanded you to observe the Sabbath day.

There are more references to the sanctity of the seventh day throughout the entire Tanakh (Old Testament).

I went to the trouble of pasting these in because a list of references would not suffice. Understand, Yahweh speaks NO superfluous words. We are to be fed by every word from the mouth of God.

We MUST understand how monumentally important this day is to HIM. He is very precise in reiterating this command on multiple occasions...

Now, if Yahweh does not change and He does NOTHING without first revealing it to the prophets... Where is it prophesied that the eternally ordained day of rest would change? Where?

Truth? There is NO prophecy telling it would change. In fact, exactly the opposite is true! It is prophesied that we will celebrate the Sabbath in the New Heaven and New Earth! Speaking of the Eternal Kingdom, He says,

Isaiah 66:22-23
"For just as the **new heavens and the new earth** which I make will endure before Me," declares the Lord, "So your offspring and your name will endure. And it shall be from new moon to new moon and from Sabbath to Sabbath, all mankind will come to bow down before Me," says the Lord.

Further, He calls the Two Witnesses. The same Two Witnesses used in multiple places to evidence that His Commandments are still in place!

Yeshua, testifying of the same Two Witnesses says,

Matthew 5:17-19
Do not think that I came to abolish the Law or the Prophets; I did not come to abolish but to fulfill. For truly I say to you, until **heaven and earth** pass away, not the smallest letter or stroke shall pass from the Law until all is accomplished. Whoever then annuls one of the least of these commandments, and teaches others to do the same, shall be called least in the kingdom of heaven; but whoever keeps and teaches them, he shall be called great in the kingdom of heaven.

I ask again, 'Where is it prophesied that the day of rest would change?' Yeshua says the Law remains the same until heaven and earth pass away!

Or, another way, with the command being so clearly stated on no less than six occasions in the Torah, where is even one equally clear retraction or stated change of the commandment?

All of the apostles taught on the Sabbath. Even when teaching Gentiles. Acts 13:42-44 is a great example. Even given the opportunity to preach at other times, Paul and Barnabas choose the next Sabbath.

Nowhere, ever, in Scripture is another day taught or exampled. Period. (Someone will bring up the Acts 20:7 phrase 'first day of the week,' previously covered in this chapter. Before you get ambushed, I'd advise looking up the verse in Greek... It says (transliterated) 'mia ton sabbaton'. If you believe that means 'first day of the week,' I have a bridge for sale in San Fran...)

Bottom line: The Word NEVER teaches anything but Sabbath keeping. It was Constantine and the Bishop of Rome that countermanded Yahweh's Word and led all of Christendom, by the edge of a sword, into Sunday-keeping.

The Roman Catholic Church, on Sunday worship, in their own words:

> [Protestants] deem it their duty to keep the Sunday holy. Why? Because the Catholic Church tells them to do so. They have no other reason...The observance of Sunday thus comes to be an ecclesiastical law entirely distinct from the divine law of Sabbath observance...The author of the Sunday law...is the Catholic Church.
> -   Ecclesiastical Review, February 1914

> The Sunday...is purely a creation of the Catholic Church.
> -   American Catholic Quarterly Review, January 1883

> Sunday...is the law of the Catholic Church alone....
> -   American Sentinel (Catholic), June 1893

Sunday is a Catholic institution and its claim to observance can be defended only on Catholic principles... From beginning to end of Scripture there is not a single passage that warrants the transfer of weekly public worship from the last day of the week to the first.

-    Catholic Press, Sydney, Australia, August 1900

It is well to remind the Presbyterians, Baptists, Methodists, and all other Christians, that the Bible does not support them anywhere in their observance of Sunday. Sunday is an institution of the Roman Catholic Church, and those who observe the day observe a commandment of the Catholic Church.

- Priest Brady, in an address reported in *The News*, Elizabeth, New Jersey, March 18, 1903

From this we may understand how great is the authority of the church in interpreting or explaining to us the commandments of God – an authority which is acknowledged by the universal practice of the whole Christian world, even of those sects which profess to take the holy Scriptures as their sole rule of faith, since they observe as the day of rest not the seventh day of the week demanded by the Bible, but the first day. Which we know is to be kept holy, only from the tradition and teaching of the Catholic church.

-    Henry Gibson, *Catechism Made Easy*, #2, 9th edition, vol.1, p. 341-342.

It was the Catholic church which...has transferred this rest to Sunday in remembrance of the resurrection of our Lord. Therefore the observance of Sunday by the Protestants is an homage they pay, in spite of themselves, to the authority of the (Catholic) church.

-    Monsignor Louis Segur, *Plain Talk About the Protestantism of Today*, p. 213.

Sunday is our mark or authority...the church is above the Bible, and this transference of Sabbath observance is proof of that fact.
- *Catholic Record* of London, Ontario, September 1, 1923.

"Of course the Catholic Church claims that the change (Saturday Sabbath to Sunday) was her act...And the act is a mark of her ecclesiastical authority in religious things." H.F. Thomas, Chancellor of Cardinal Gibbons.

I have repeatedly offered $1,000 to anyone who can prove to me from the Bible alone that I am bound to keep Sunday holy. There is no such law in the Bible. It is a law of the holy Catholic Church alone. The Bible says, 'Remember the Sabbath day to keep it holy.' The Catholic Church says: 'No. By my divine power I abolish the Sabbath day and command you to keep holy the first day of the week.' And lo! The entire civilized world bows down in a reverent obedience to the command of the holy Catholic Church.
- Father T. Enright, C.SS.R. of the Redemptoral College, Kansas City, in a lecture at Hartford, Kansas, February 18, 1884, printed in *History of the Sabbath*, p. 802.

Protestants... accept Sunday rather than Saturday as the day for public worship after the Catholic Church made the change... But the Protestant mind does not seem to realize that... In observing the Sunday, they are accepting the authority of the spokesman for the church, the Pope.
- *Our Sunday Visitor*, February 15, 1950.

Again, I ask: Where is the Day of Rest, ordained from the week of creation, changed from the seventh day?

If there is NO change in Scripture of the Day, then who countermanded the Almighty? Are you following the commandment or a tradition?

Walk as Yeshua walked. Keep the Sabbath. Blessings follow obedience.

4 PARADIGM SHIFTERS

The outer layer of the earth's crust is formed of large plates, called tectonic plates, that move. The regions where the plates rub against each other are called fault lines and predictably, as the plates shift, friction along the fault lines is stored up until some tiny movement causes the plates to suddenly and violently snap toward a position of relief. This snap, or earthquake comes with no warning, radically shaking the ground and sometimes even reshaping the landscape.

Mounting evidence contrary to our established thought patterns rarely leads to gradual change. What more often happens is a sudden and massive shift, much like an earthquake. This is called a paradigm shift. Essentially, bits of mounting evidence that challenge our established thought pattern begin building up until we suddenly find that we have a new thought pattern that more accurately reflects what we know to be true.

Following are a couple posts that reveal verses and concepts that, when evaluated, will shift our thought process and bring us into more Biblical alignment. I titled these 'paradigm-shifting' thoughts and verses because they can shake up long held beliefs that may not be entirely true.

Enjoy and study each of these verses. They may bring change, but with it they draw us closer to the fullness of Truth!

10 Paradigm-shifting New Testament Verses

Originally posted on November 9, 2013.

Maybe I'm the only person this happens to, but have you ever read a verse that you've read a 100 times, but suddenly you 'see' it totally differently? Like a bolt of lightning, or a V-8 moment, you suddenly understand it in a whole new light?

An optical example is at the left… Do you see a young woman, or an old woman?

Sometimes seeing one can become an impediment to seeing the other, yet both are cleverly there.

Theologically, we can be told a certain paradigm or traditional understanding so many times that we can't 'see' something else that is obviously there. Yet, taking time to ponder and refocus, can suddenly open whole new worlds of understanding that utterly shift our paradigm.

Here are ten such New Testament verses that are paradigm shifters. I pray you are as challenged as I was the first time these verses 'hit' me. They open doors to big blessings.

1. Jesus/Yeshua said,

   Matthew 5:19
   Whoever then annuls one of the least of these commandments, and teaches others to do the same, shall be called least in the kingdom of heaven; but whoever keeps and teaches them, he shall be called great in the kingdom of heaven.

Right here, Yeshua tells us exactly how to be LEAST in the kingdom. Ever notice that? He says, "Here's how to be Least in the Kingdom, annul one of the least of the commandments and teach others to do the same."

Who wants to be LEAST in the kingdom? Any takers? No hands?

Believe it or not, 99% of all Christian denominations, from Rome to the uttermost parts of the earth, teach not that 'least commandments' are 'done away with' but whole chapters no longer apply. Most Reformed Presbyterian denominations abide by the Westminster Confession of Faith. Chapter XIX, iii says, "All which ceremonial laws are now abrogated, under the New Testament." The dictionary says that 'abrogated' means 'annulled,' therefore this document, drafted by men directly contradicts the words of Yeshua.

Whom do we believe? The Westminster divines? Or, the Divine Messiah?

Do we want to be LEAST in the kingdom? Or, GREAT? Hmmm . . . seems like a no-brainer, but then verses like this one demand that we use our brain and swim against the tide of theological tradition. This requires a paradigm shift!

2. In Acts chapters 6 and 7 we read the story of the first martyr, Stephen. Have you ever paid attention to why he was martyred? Exactly how did he wind up before the Sanhedrin? This verse will shake up some theology.

Act 6:13-14
They put forward false witnesses who said, "This man incessantly speaks against this holy place and the Law; for we have heard him say that this Nazarene, Jesus, will destroy this place and alter the customs which Moses handed down to us." Acts 6:13-14

Stephen was stoned to death for 'teaching against the Temple and against the Torah!' HOWEVER, the Sanhedrin had to use false witnesses to bring the charges. False witnesses!! Let that sink in.

Do you know what that means? Yep, it means Stephen, a man filled with the Holy Spirit, in the months or year immediately following the resurrection of Messiah was NOT teaching against the Law. In fact, he was zealous for Moses as we'll see in a minute.

Ironically, 99% of Christendom today could be charged with 'teaching against the Temple and the Torah' and the charges would be TRUE! Hmmm. . . .

By implication of the testimony of these false witnesses, Yeshua did NOT "alter the customs which Moses handed down to us." Paradigm shifter!

3. The Apostle Paul, in coming up to Jerusalem to give a report, tells of the wonders being worked in Asia Minor among the Gentiles. Acts 21:20 relates to us the excited response about those who believed in Jerusalem,

Acts 21:20
And when they heard it they began glorifying God; and they said to him, "You see, brother, how many thousands there are among the Jews of those who have believed, and they are all zealous for the Law."

Belief in Messiah does not negate or nullify the Torah. Rather, it should increase our zeal for obedience out of love!

Here's a question: Do theologians, 1000 to 2000 years removed from Jerusalem and the Apostles know more than James and Paul and all the elders who are standing here witnessing this meeting? I didn't think so. This verse is paradigm-shifting.

4. Just a couple verses later may be the single most shocking verse in the New Testament for most Christians. As a pastor, when I read and fully understood this verse, it totally rocked my world.

Acts 21:26

Then Paul took the men, and the next day, purifying himself along with them, went into the temple giving notice of the completion of the days of purification, until the sacrifice was offered for each one of them.

Yep, you just read that Paul, the Apostle and possible author of Hebrews, was 'in the temple' offering 'sacrifices' some 20+ years after the Damascus road experience. He was seized, not for offering sacrifices, but for 'allegedly' bringing Gentiles into the Temple courts. (False witnesses again!)

Paul was offering sacrifices in the Temple. Ponder the significance to most theology that says 'the sacrificial system has been done away with'. Yes, this is really heavy, but it is a reality in Scripture that MUST be dealt with. Zechariah 14:21 speaks of future sacrifices. So does Ezekiel 43 and 44. Parts of Isaiah allude to the same. Sacrifices in the future is a challenging and paradigm-shifting topic.

5. Having read and wrestled with the previous question, many come to the conclusion that Paul was just acting according to custom and meant no theological harm. While this would make him out to be a liar, let's just go to one of four of his legal testimonies,

Acts 25:7-8
After Paul arrived, the Jews who had come down from Jerusalem stood around him, bringing many and serious charges against him which they could not prove, while Paul said in his own defense, "I have committed no offense either against the Law of the Jews or against the temple or against Caesar."

Ahhh, the presence of false witnesses. Paul, by his own testimony clearly states that he has not committed offense against the Torah or the Temple.

Either, he is lying, or he is telling the truth.

If Paul is lying, can we trust anything else he has written?

If he is telling the truth, how can we claim he taught against the Law?

Teaching against the Torah is an offense against the Torah that is punishable by death!! Cue Deuteronomy 12:32-13:11!

Seriously, if Paul was teaching against the Torah, why didn't his accusers simply go get a copy of the letter to the Galatians? According to Christendom it was his defining work against the Torah! There's all the proof his accusers needed... And, just for the record, that was a letter he likely wrote before Acts 15, therefore, it was widely available to his accusers in the nearly ten years prior to his arrest.

Long story short, Galatians is NOT about 'doing away with the Law.' It is about the misuse of the Law for salvation. ["I do not think it means what you think it means!" – from *The Princess Bride*]

Paul says, 'I have committed no offense against either the Law of the Jews or against the Temple.' Ponder deeply. No offense against the Law. Paradigm-shifter.

6. Paul wrote many of the epistles and often verses are taken out of context to prove an antinomian, or 'anti-Torah,' bias. Here is something the Apostle Paul said that theologians love to ignore or completely tap dance around,

Acts 3:31
Do we then nullify the Law through faith? May it never be! On the contrary, we establish the Law.

In one verse, Paul declares, 'through faith we establish the Law, we do not nullify it!'

Most Pauline theology (mis)uses proof texts to demonstrate that he 'did away with the Law.' Yet, Paul affirms the Torah over and over. If in some passages he overturns the Law and in others he affirms the Law, then we have a schizophrenic Apostle on the loose!!

Maybe, just maybe, we have misunderstood or willfully misused some of his writing to be stiff-necked and rebellious just like our fathers!!

Meditate on this: Paul said, 'By faith we establish the Law.' Paradigm-shifter.

7. So how did Paul ever get so misunderstood and 'whacked out?' The Apostle Peter tells us and issues a warning,

2 Peter 3:15-17
Bear in mind that our Lord's patience means salvation, just as our dear brother Paul also wrote you with the wisdom that God gave him. He writes the same way in all his letters, speaking in them of these matters. His letters contain some things that are hard to understand, which ignorant and unstable people distort, as they do the other Scriptures, to their own destruction. Therefore, dear friends, since you have been forewarned, be on your guard so that you may not be carried away by the error of the lawless and fall from your secure position.

Peter tells us plainly,
- Paul's letters can be hard to understand
- the ignorant and unstable distort him
- the result is lawLESSness

We would easily agree that Paul can be hard to understand, but what does this verse mean by 'ignorant and unstable?'

The ignorant and the unstable are those who do not have a firm foundation in the Torah. Other translations call them 'unlearned' or 'untaught.'

We have already seen that Paul upheld the Torah and we see here that the error these 'unlearned' teach leads to lawlessness! Paul was steeped in the Torah and was zealous for the Torah. He would not dare or even dream of teaching against the 'perfect Torah.'

The error of twisting Paul is lawLESSness. Does modern theology teach lawFULness, or lawLESSness? Does your understanding of Paul lead to lawfulness or lawlessness?

Peter warns, 'be on your guard that you not be carried away by the error of the lawless!' Paradigm-shift ahead!

8. In fact, what is the error of lawlessness?

I John 3:4
Everyone who practices sin also practices lawlessness; and sin is lawlessness.

The Law, the Torah, defines sin. Breaking the Law is sin. Therefore, lawlessness IS sin.

'Doing away with the Law' is doing away with the definition of sin, and indeed, the act is sin itself!
- Annul a commandment? Sin.
- Teach against the commandments? Sin.
- Avoid/ignore the commandments? Sin.

See? This is why Yeshua could NOT have changed the Law or abolished anything, before or after His atoning sacrifice. Doing so would be sin!

Paradigm-shifting.

9. Yeshua did not change the Law! How do we know besides His own declaration that 'I did not come to abolish the Law?' The author of Hebrews declares,

Hebrews 13:8
Jesus Christ is the same yesterday and today and forever.

The Apostle John tells us that Yeshua is the Word and He was in the beginning. A study of the Rabbinic understanding of the Messiah being the Word, or Memra, reveals the clear connection that not only was Yeshua present at creation, but He was present at Mount Sinai and likely was the One who met Moshe on the Mountain. Thus, He gave the Torah!!

He is 'the same yesterday and today and forever!' When we truly understand His eternality and involvement at every level of Scripture, then we realize, the Memra, the Word doesn't change. The Law doesn't change.

Isn't that what Yeshua said? 'Until heaven and earth pass away not one jot or tittle will pass from the Law and the prophets?'

Not one jot!! Not a single consonant! Not ONE!! Paradigm-shift!

10. What we absolutely have to come to grips with is that Yeshua and the Father are One (echad/united). They are not in opposition. Yeshua ONLY taught what the Father gave Him and nowhere is the Law ever prophesied to be done away with or in any way reduced. Never!

Yeshua said,

John 7:16
My doctrine is not mine, but his that sent me.

Yeshua ONLY taught the Word of His Father.

Time for a paradigm shift!

There are many, many more verses that support what we have seen here in this post... These are not isolated, cherry-picked verses, but they reveal the need to re-evaluate the errant doctrines and traditions of men that teach against the Torah.

"Be on guard that you not be carried away by the error of lawless men!!"

10 Paradigm-shifting Old Testament Verses

Originally posted on November 16, 2013.

Discussion and thinking are VERY important. Most people simply accept what they are told by their parents and/or the pulpit and they never question the establishment. Frankly, when we each stand before the Judge, He is not going to see if we adhered to what our parents or denomination believed. He is going to judge by His standard, Scripture, and we are each accountable for what we have in our hand, even if we choose not to study it.

Since we looked at NT verses, it is only fair to consider some 'Old Testament' paradigm-shifting verses. The great challenge is that there are about five times as many verses to choose from, so whittling the list down to just ten is hard, but here goes.

I have written about a number of these verse at one point or another, so I would encourage finding this post on natsab.com and following links if a particular topic piques your interest or challenges your paradigm.

1. Isaiah 40:8 is an oft quoted verse, especially from the pulpit, but I really wonder if we stop and ponder the magnitude!!

Isaiah 40:8
The grass withers, the flower fades, but the word of our God stands forever.

'The word of our God stands forever.' Forever!

Doctrines and traditional theological understanding are quick to declare parts of God's Word are 'done away with.' That is really hard to square with 'the word of our God stands forever.' Yeshua told us that 'not one jot or tittle would pass from the Law and the Prophets until heaven and earth pass away.' Kinda sounds like, 'the word of our God stands forever.'

But, there are entire denominations that declare certain parts of God's eternal/everlasting Word to be 'annulled' or 'abrogated.' I've even heard pastors in those denominations read Scripture, then recite this verse before preaching from their text.

Hmmm. . . . Irony. Wonder if they ever stop to think about what they say if they are preaching that some part of God's Law is 'done away with?'

The Word of our God says, 'the word of our God stands forever.' When we fully understand what that sentence says, it is paradigm-shifting.

2. Abraham believed God and it was credited to him as righteousness. True . . . but that is not the paradigm shifter.

The Apostle Paul had to remind his readers of this fact when establishing the importance of salvation by faith. They fully understood the rest of the story.

Today, we are unfamiliar with the rest of the story, so here it is,

Genesis 26:4-5
[Yahweh, speaking to Isaac] I will multiply your descendants as the stars of heaven, and will give your descendants all these lands; and by your descendants all the nations of the earth shall be blessed; 5 because Abraham obeyed Me and kept My charge, My commandments, My statutes and My laws (torah)."

Because!

Faith without works is dead! Faith opens the door. Faith lets us into the family. But, obedience then evidences that faith. Lack of obedience equals NO faith. Period!

Modern theology's easy believism and endless free grace is appalling. They are poor excuses to allow the trampling of God's commandments and expectations.

Understanding that Abraham had and kept Torah is a real boggler that totally flies in the face of Christian theology that says, 'Abraham just believed.'

"because Abraham obeyed Me and kept My charge, My commandments, My statutes and My laws (torah). . ."

Paradigm-shifter.

3. More than once, since beginning to keep more of my King's commandments, I have had well-meaning Christians tell me that trying to keep the commands would lead to death and judgment – that I had to 'live by them' – never mind that they misquote Paul's use of Torah and twist it to say exactly the opposite of what it says.

In fact, the Torah says that observing the commandments leads to righteousness and life!!

Deuteronomy 6:25
It will be righteousness for us if we are careful to observe all this commandment before the Lord our God, just as He commanded us.

Why wouldn't we want to keep the Torah?! It is the definition of righteousness and God's desire for how we are to live!

Today, Christendom loves to denigrate the Torah. 'Set free from the Law' they say, but Yahweh promises to bless those who are obedient. Hmmm. . . .

"It will be righteousness for us. . . ."

Paradigm-shifting.

4. 'God's not interested in actions! He's interested in the heart! Don't you know anything?'

Yeah, Christendom seems to think that something changed at the cross and that the heart became more important. Guess they never read,

Deuteronomy 5:29

Oh that they had such a heart in them, that they would fear Me and keep all My commandments always, that it may be well with them and with their sons forever!

Yep. A circumcised heart is a Torah concept. The Father's desire has ALWAYS been a circumcised heart. But, a circumcised heart will lead to obedience – to 'keep[ing] all My commandments . . . forever.'

No surprise there if you know your Bible. See Ezekiel 37:24-28.

So, 'the Word of our God [that] stands forever' says, 'Oh that they had such a heart in them, that they would fear Me and keep all My commandments always. . . .'

That'll shake up the 'law has been done away with' paradigm.

5. Be ye holy! The Apostle Peter speaks of holiness and quotes a passage from the Torah.

Ever looked it up? It'll shift your paradigm!

Leviticus 11:44-45
For I am the Lord your God. Consecrate yourselves therefore, and be holy, for I am holy. And you shall not make yourselves unclean with any of the swarming things that swarm on the earth. For I am the Lord who brought you up from the land of Egypt to be your God; thus you shall be holy, for I am holy.

While we all agree that holiness is a concept throughout Scripture, do we understand that Yahweh gives several specific marks or 'works' that lead to holiness? The above quoted passage is one of them . . . but we have to read the larger context.

Here is the Pete Rambo condensed version, since many will not take the time to read the whole passage,
- Eat the clean animals.
- DO NOT eat the unclean animals – they are detestable!!
- Be ye holy for I am holy.

- Learn the difference in the clean and the unclean, between the edible and the detestable. Leviticus 11

Nowhere has Yahweh's standard of holiness ever changed, nor has His definition of food ever changed. Simply, swine were detestable then, they are now and will be on judgment day according to Isaiah 66:16-17! (Some might say Peter's Vision in Acts 10 changed the food laws, but that vision is defined for us by Acts 10:28. The vision is not about food.)

One aspect of holiness, according to the word of our God that stands forever, is what we eat. That thought is a wrench in the middle of lawless theology. Paradigm shift!

6. Somehow the word 'forever' and 'perpetual' means nothing to Christendom.

Seriously! It seems that deep thinking theologians have WAY more trouble with 'forever' than third-graders!

Put your 'third-grader glasses on' and read these verses and then we'll have a test. A piece of candy if you get the answer right!

It is to be a perpetual statute throughout your generations in all your dwelling places.

It is to be a perpetual statute in all your dwelling places throughout your generations.

It is to be a perpetual statute throughout your generations in all your dwelling places.

It shall be a perpetual statute throughout your generations

True or False: The statute(s) referred to by these verses ended at the cross.

If you said 'True,' you are in the company of the Roman Catholic Church, Martin Luther, John Calvin, John Bunyan, and a billion Christians . . . and you are wrong. Period.

The verses all come from Leviticus 23. This chapter details the 'Feasts of the Lord,' and we are told multiple times throughout the chapter that the feasts are perpetual statutes, throughout your generations, in all your dwellings. That kinda sounds like, 'til heaven and earth pass away.' Yes?

Also, for those that like to argue that 'the law only applies in the land of Israel,' the phrase 'in all your dwelling places' puts the kibosh on that error.

Honestly, Scripture only requires about a fifth grade education to get the important parts. It is the theologians doing mental gymnastics trying to find ways to justify lawlessness that cause trouble.

'Forever' and 'perpetual' mean forever. Blindingly obvious. I know. But for some, this is paradigm-shifting!

7. Since we are talking about 'forever' and 'perpetual' as well as 'throughout your generations' and 'in all your dwellings,' here is another one that just rocks the whole Christendom theological world:

Exodus 31:12-13, 16-17
The Lord spoke to Moses, saying, "But as for you, speak to the sons of Israel, saying, 'You shall surely observe My Sabbaths; for this is a sign between Me and you throughout your generations, that you may know that I am the Lord who sanctifies you. . . .

So the sons of Israel shall observe the Sabbath, to celebrate the Sabbath throughout their generations as a perpetual covenant.' It is a sign between Me and the sons of Israel forever; for in six days the Lord made heaven and earth, but on the seventh day He ceased from labor, and was refreshed."

Oh, and 'the word of our God that stands forever' says that keeping the Sabbath is a sanctification issue. Hmmm. For MUCH more on the Sabbath issue, natsab.com has a paper my then 16 year old son wrote. It bears studying.

For those who might focus on 'sons of Israel,' I would recommend re-reading Ephesians 2:12 until you understand what it means to be grafted in.

This particular topic is deeply challenging, but the truth will set you free. Simply, the day of worship, designated in the Garden of Eden before Adam and Eve sinned was the seventh day Sabbath. Yeshua kept the seventh-day Sabbath. Nowhere are we ever commanded, or is it ever even implied, that the day of worship was changed by God.

The Word says, "So the sons of Israel shall observe the Sabbath, to celebrate the Sabbath throughout their generations as a perpetual (olam) covenant." Paradigm-shifting!

8. We've talked about the fact that the word of our God stands forever. His word also says we are not to add or subtract from that word. Interestingly, it says that in a particularly important place:

Deuteronomy 12:32-13:5
Whatever I command you, you shall be careful to do; you shall not add to nor take away from it.
If a prophet or a dreamer of dreams arises among you and gives you a sign or a wonder, and the sign or the wonder comes true, concerning which he spoke to you, saying, 'Let us go after other gods (whom you have not known) and let us serve them,' you shall not listen to the words of that prophet or that dreamer of dreams; for the Lord your God is testing you to find out if you love the Lord your God with all your heart and with all your soul. You shall follow the Lord your God and fear Him; and you shall keep His commandments, listen to His voice, serve Him, and cling to Him. But that prophet or that dreamer of dreams shall be put to death, because he has counseled rebellion against the Lord your God who brought you from the land of Egypt and redeemed you from the house of slavery, to seduce you from the way in which the Lord your God commanded

you to walk. So you shall purge the evil from among you.

Simply, neither Yeshua/Jesus nor Sha'ul/Paul had any desire or authority to change, add to or take away from the commandments of God. Doing so would have been sin.

Both addressed the many traditions and oral law that had been added by the rabbis, but neither ever overturned a single 'jot or tittle' from the Torah. Study for yourself and find this to be true! It will totally shift your paradigm!

9. By now, many who read this chapter are a bit confused and scratching their heads. Obviously, what you are seeing here is not what you've been taught from the pulpit. I understand; I was in your shoes a couple years ago!

Let's look at a couple more verses from the 'word of our God [that] stands forever.'

Psalm 97:7-13
The Torah of the Lord is perfect, restoring the soul;
The testimony of the Lord is sure, making wise the simple.
The precepts of the Lord are right, rejoicing the heart;
The commandment of the Lord is pure, enlightening the eyes.
The fear of the Lord is clean, enduring forever;
The judgments of the Lord are true; they are righteous altogether.
They are more desirable than gold, yes, than much fine gold;
Sweeter also than honey and the drippings of the honeycomb.
Moreover, by them Your servant is warned; In keeping them there is great reward.

Or, the Pete Rambo condensed version is,
* The Torah of the Lord is perfect, restoring the soul;
* In keeping Torah there is great reward.

When did this verse (these verses) stop being true? Isn't this the word of our God that stands forever?

Ponder this thought deeply:

The Torah is perfect instruction in righteousness that leads to great reward!

That really shakes up the theology of Christendom as regards the Torah! Here is a deeper look into this passage and its implications. It shifts the ole' paradigm.

10. Read Psalm 119. The whole thing. Bask in the deep love and respect the author of the Psalm has for God's Law. The commandments, the ordinances, the precepts, the statutes, etc.

Before my eyes were opened, this was one of the most difficult and boring passages of Scripture in the Bible. Seriously.

After the Father opened my eyes to the great wonder of His majesty as revealed in His instructions (Torah) for how to live righteously, this Psalm became a glorious source of joy! I remember taking the time to highlight every synonym of 'law' and 'precepts'. I got out my concordance to identify and circle in another color every occurrence of the word 'Torah.' I highlighted in still another color whole verses that held special revelation contrary to accepted Christian doctrine.

Here are a couple favorites – verses so rich and deep that they are delicious on the tongue. Candy for the mind. . . .

How blessed are those whose way is blameless, who walk in the Torah of the Lord.
So I will keep Your Torah continually, forever and ever.
And I will walk at liberty, for I seek Your precepts.
I have inclined my heart to perform Your statutes forever, even to the end. I hate those who are double-minded, but I love Your Torah.
The sum of Your word is truth, and every one of Your righteous ordinances is everlasting.

Those who love Your Torah have great peace, and nothing causes them to stumble.
I hope for Your Yeshua, O Lord, and do Your commandments.
I long for Your Yeshua [Salvation], O Lord, and Your Torah is my delight.

Those and many others in this Psalm alone completely shatter any idea that the Torah is 'done away with.' Any doctrinal statement, pastor, teacher or church 'father' who teaches that the Law is done away with proves themselves to be utterly false.

Utterly false!

"So I will keep Your torah continually, forever and ever.
And I will walk at liberty,"

Paradigm shifter!

Do you really know the Word of the Lord? Do you really understand what 'forever' means?

I would challenge you to take off the denominational glasses and get before Yahweh and open your heart. Read His Word that stands forever and accept what it says without filtering through doctrinal statements. Be willing to contend for truth!

5 WHAT ABOUT JESUS?

As God, by His Holy Spirit, began to open my eyes to falsehoods in my belief system, I began to understand that His everlasting, unchanging Word promises so many blessings for simple obedience to His Torah. At the same time, I began to wonder that if all of this were true, then it somehow had to mesh with what I knew to be true about Jesus/Yeshua the Messiah. As a pastor, I had always believed that Jesus could be found throughout the 'Old' Testament, but now I had to set out and really prove that.

Here are a few posts and a study guide that will prompt much thought for you as you begin to explore how the Torah and Yeshua fit together. Indeed, He is revealed on every page in multiple ways. Best of all, the pieces fit so much better than I ever imagined.

These entries will not answer your every question, they might even create some questions, but I believe they will set you on a course that will help you better understand who our Messiah is and how He is revealed over and over.

I begin with one of the most viewed articles I ever wrote:

Was Jesus on Mt. Sinai? Does it matter?

Originally posted on December 4, 2013.

Here is an interesting question that reveals a theological/doctrinal conundrum for most of Christendom:

Was Jesus on Mt. Sinai?

Before answering that question, let's consider what all of normative believers in Messiah know to be truth,

John 1:1-3
In the beginning was the Word, and the Word was with God, and the Word was God. He was in the beginning with God. All things came into being through Him, and apart from Him nothing came into being that has come into being.

And,

Colossians 1:16-17
For by Him all things were created, both in the heavens and on earth, visible and invisible, whether thrones or dominions or rulers or authorities—all things have been created through Him and for Him. He is before all things, and in Him all things hold together.

Clearly, the Messiah was present at or, actually, before Creation!

Even the authoritative Aramaic translation of the Torah, Targum Onkelos, reads,

Genesis 3:8
And they heard the voice of the **Word of the Lord God** walking in the garden in the evening of the day. . . .

Genesis 15:6
Behold now the heavens, and number the stars, if thou art able to number them; and He said to him, So will be thy sons. And **he believed in the Word of the Lord**,

104

(Memra da Yeya,) and He reckoned it to him unto justification.

It acknowledges the presence of 'the Word of the Lord' at Creation and in dozens of other places in the Torah!

So, Was Jesus/Yeshua at Mt. Sinai?

Let's consider one other concept, before answering.

Even if they do not always agree on the finer points of the 'echad' (one/united) nature of the Father and the Son, Christendom widely regards Jesus/Yeshua as being of the same essence, and in perfect unity with the Father.

Messianic Rabbi Itzhak Shapira would argue for Yeshua as a 'manifestation of the Father,' demonstrating one perspective of the connection between Father and Son from a very Judaic source.

The bottom line is that even Yeshua said, 'I and the Father are one,' and 'If you have seen Me, you have seen the Father.'

So, knowing that Jesus/Yeshua was at Creation and acknowledging His unity with the Father, was He at Mt. Sinai during the giving of the Torah?

Frankly, that seems like a total 'no-brainer,' but prior to digging deeper in the Scriptures, I'm not sure I ever contemplated the answer, or more importantly, the implications!!

Consider Exodus 24:9-11,

Exodus 24:9-11
Then Moses went up with Aaron, Nadab and Abihu, and seventy of the elders of Israel, and **they saw the God of Israel;** and under His feet there appeared to be a pavement of sapphire, as clear as the sky itself. Yet He did not stretch out His hand against the nobles of the sons of Israel; and they saw God, and they ate and drank.

Besides having this wonderful flavor of the Divine Holy One desiring so much to be with His people and seeing that desire manifest again at the 'Last Supper' as He eats with His disciples, this is an amazing account of humans in the presence of the Living God.

BUT, can humans see God the Father face to face?

John 1:18
No one has seen God at any time; the only begotten God who is in the bosom of the Father, He has explained Him.

And,

John 6:46
Not that anyone has seen the Father, except the One who is from God; He has seen the Father.

I think it is clear from multiple angles that Jesus/Yeshua was on Mt. Sinai, and He is the One Moses spoke with and the elders ate with.

Why is this significant?

Well, the Torah, God's instructions, sometimes called 'Law,' was given on Mt. Sinai and Moses knew God face to face. Additionally, parts of the Torah were spoken from the Mountain directly to Israel. Targum Onkelos translates Exodus 19:16-17 as,

Exodus 19:16-17
And it was the third day at morning; and there were voices, and lightnings, and mighty clouds upon the mountain, and the voice of the trumpet exceedingly strong; and all the people trembled who were in the camp. And Moshe led forth the people out of the camp **to meet the Word of the Lord**; and they stood at the lower parts of the mount.

Jesus/Yeshua gave the Law!

Let that sink in!

Yeshua gave the Law!!!

This poses a sizable conundrum for most of Christendom that argues that Jesus 'did away with the Law.'

The theological and doctrinal implications are staggering.

Yeshua also said,

John 14:15
If you love Me, you will keep My commandments.

Ponder the sheer gravity of that statement and its implications!

Do you know what His commandments really are?

Got Torah?

_____

Other related thoughts: James 4:12 refers to Yeshua as the Lawgiver, a clear affirmation of His being on Mt. Sinai.

Could Yeshua die for a covenant His Father made? Or, was He 'sent' before the covenant was made, and was HE the One who made the covenant with Israel, the Bride?

Who walked through the pieces at the Abrahamic Covenant? Gen. 15:1 says 'the Word of the Lord' came to Abram... Did Yeshua make that covenant as well? (I think so!)

_____

And, a personal aside: Pondering this is so HUGE, that it makes me giddy with excitement and filled with a holy fear/dread all at the same time! No wonder Rav Sha'ul would burst into praise saying,

Romans 11:33-36
Oh, the depth of the riches both of the wisdom and knowledge of God! How unsearchable are His judgments and unfathomable His ways! For who has

known the mind of the Lord, or who became His counselor? Or who has first given to Him that it might be paid back to him again? For from Him and through Him and to Him are all things. To Him be the glory forever. Amen.

Was Jesus on Mt. Sinai? Part 2

Originally posted on January 17, 2015.

"Was Jesus on Mt Sinai? Does it matter?" is one of the most popular and most shared posts ever on my blog. In that post I articulated and defended from several angles my conviction that Yeshua (Jesus) stood on Mt. Sinai and was/is the Lawgiver with whom Moshe spoke.

I had been asked to teach a series at a local Baptist Church demonstrating Yeshua's presence in the Tanach (OT). We began with the 'Angel of the Lord' instances to reveal Him as the physical, visible manifestation of Elohim (God).

Soon after I began teaching this series, in the middle of our Shabbat midrash at our home fellowship my attention was drawn to chase a 'rabbi trail' that led to me reading a verse I've seen a dozen times. You already know the rest of the story: I saw something I had not noticed before...

In Stephen's defense before the Sanhedrin, Acts 7, he says something that is a stunner,

Acts 7:37-38
This is the Moses who said to the sons of Israel, 'God will raise up for you a prophet like me from your brethren.' This is the one who was in the congregation in the wilderness together with **the angel who was speaking to him on Mount Sinai**, and who was with our fathers; and he received living oracles to pass on to you.

Checkmate!

Stephen says it was the Angel of Yehovah (Lord) who spoke with Moshe on Mt. Sinai. Simple math demonstrates that the Angel of the Lord is Yeshua.

the angel who was speaking to him on Mount Sinai,

John 14:15
If you love Me, you will keep My commandments.

Any questions?

Well, earlier I had done considerable research into the Angel of the Lord. I will share a study guide I developed, but first I want to share another much read post that begins to explore the topic.

What did Moses see in the 'Burning Bush?'

Originally posted on December 12, 2013.

The first part of Exodus chapter three details Moses' encounter with the 'burning bush.' I re-read this portion of Scripture the other day as part of a recent topical study when I saw something I had never seen before.

Moses tells us precisely what he saw in the burning bush.

I shared what I found at my Torah Study and, with more than 350 years of 'Bible knowledge' among the seven of us, not one of us had ever noticed what Moses saw in the burning bush. That alone was an interesting lesson in how our paradigms can be shaped, even when the text is startlingly specific.

So, what exactly did Moses see? Let's read the first five verses:

Exodus 3:1-5
Now Moses was pasturing the flock of Jethro his father-in-law, the priest of Midian; and he led the flock to the west side of the wilderness and came to Horeb, the mountain of God. The angel of the Lord appeared to him in a blazing fire from the midst of a bush; and he looked, and behold, the bush was burning with fire, yet the bush was not consumed. So Moses said, "I must turn aside now and see this marvelous sight, why the bush is not burned up." When the Lord saw that he turned aside to look, God called to him from the midst of the bush and said, "Moses, Moses!" And he said, "Here I am." Then He said, "Do not come near here; remove your sandals from your feet, for the place on which you are standing is holy ground."

Did you see it?

Even upon reading the passage out loud, our group missed it. In fact, the only reason I noticed it is because I was on a mission reading every mention of 'the Angel of the Lord' in the Tanak. And, BANG! There it is!

A better question is, "WHO did Moses see in the burning bush?"

The timing for seeing this could not have been better! I had just written "Was Jesus on Mt. Sinai?" The question explored has particular import in understanding His connection with the giving of the Torah and our obligation to 'keep My commandments.' So, when I read,

> **The angel of the Lord appeared to him** in a blazing fire from the midst of a bush; . . . **God called to him** from the midst of the bush and said, "Moses, Moses!"

I got excited. It is another stark proof that Yeshua (Jesus) was not only there, but intimately involved in every step, from Creation until Revelation!

Now, lest you think I am running ahead of logic, let's take a look at several of the 'Angel of the Lord' passages to verify that indeed, each is a 'Christophany' (to use an established term most are familiar with...).

John 1:18, in a passage concerning the divine nature of Yeshua the Messiah, says,

John 1:18
No one has seen God at any time; the only begotten God who is in the bosom of the Father, He has explained Him.

In saying this, John clearly teaches that ALL visible encounters with 'God' are actually Him revealing Himself in/through Yeshua. His glory is revealed to varying degrees, depending on the particular event/circumstances.

Hagar, in Genesis 16, has an amazing encounter with the Angel of the Lord and acknowledges that He is Yahweh ('the Lord'):

Genesis 16:8-15

> Now **the angel of the Lord** found her by a spring of water in the wilderness, by the spring on the way to Shur. He said, "Hagar, Sarai's maid, where have you come from and where are you going?" And she said, "I am fleeing from the presence of my mistress Sarai." Then **the angel of the Lord** said to her, "Return to your mistress, and submit yourself to her authority." Moreover, **the angel of the Lord** said to her, "I will greatly multiply your descendants so that they will be too many to count." **The angel of the Lord** said to her further, "Behold, you are with child, and you will bear a son; and you shall call his name Ishmael, because **the Lord has given heed** to your affliction. He will be a wild donkey of a man, His hand will be against everyone, and everyone's hand will be against him; and he will live to the east of all his brothers." Then she called **the name of the Lord who spoke to her**, "You are a God who sees"; for she said, "Have **I even remained alive here after seeing Him?**"

Hagar speaks with '**the angel of the Lord**' and in v. 13 it tells us that it was '**the Lord**' (YHVH) who spoke to her. Understanding John's teaching that 'no one has seen God at any time' and Hagar's amazement that she had this conversation and is still alive, we can see that Yeshua is the One she spoke with.

Another amazing 'Angel of the Lord' encounter is in Judges 13! This is an extensive encounter between Samson's mother and the Angel of the Lord followed by Manoah, her husband, praying that He return and HE DOES! Even more interesting is the connection with asking for and accepting sacrifices and worship (v. 23). Like Hagar, Manoah and his wife are afraid they will die having seen 'God' (v. 22). Read that passage in your Bible and highlight every use of 'the Angel of the Lord.' You should get about eleven!!

Let's focus on verses 17 & 18.

Judges 13:17-18

Manoah said to the angel of the Lord, "**What is your name**, so that when your words come to pass, we may honor you?" But the angel of the Lord said to him, "Why do you ask **my name**, seeing it **is wonderful**?"

The Angel of the Lord, with a wink and twist of humor, leaves a clue that will not make sense until Isaiah comes along:

Isaiah 9:6
For a child will be born to us, a son will be given to us; and the government will rest on His shoulders; and His name will be called **Wonderful** Counselor, Mighty God, Eternal Father, Prince of Peace.

I just have to laugh and marvel all at the same time. What a mighty, and humorous, God we serve! The depth of the mysteries of His Word! And, here, it clearly connects 'the Angel of the Lord' with Yeshua, the 'Wonderful Counselor!'

- There are a number of other 'Angel of the Lord' passages...
- Genesis 22, at the offering of Isaac.
- Numbers 22 has an extensive encounter with Balaam and the Angel of the Lord.
- Gideon speaks with Him in Judges 6.
- He judges David (and the people) in 2 Samuel 24:16, while destroying Sennacharib's army in Isaiah 37:36.

All interesting passages worth your time to explore.

But, in keeping with my amazement at Yeshua's appearance in the burning bush and His previously discussed presence on Mt. Sinai at the giving of the Torah, I found one other 'Angel of the Lord' appearance that cements His involvement with the Law and our need to be obedient.

Judges 2:1-5
Now **the angel of the Lord** came up from Gilgal to Bochim. And he said, "**I brought you up out of Egypt and led you** into the land which **I have sworn to your fathers**; and I said, 'I will never break **My covenant** with

you, and as for you, you shall make no covenant with the inhabitants of this land; you shall tear down their altars.' But **you have not obeyed Me**; what is this you have done? Therefore I also said, 'I will not drive them out before you; but they will become as thorns in your sides and their gods will be a snare to you.'" When **the angel of the Lord** spoke these words to **all the sons of Israel**, the people lifted up their voices and wept. So they named that place Bochim; and there they sacrificed to the Lord.

WOW!! WOW!! WOW!!

- The Angel of the Lord appears to 'all the sons of Israel!!'
- 'I brought you out of Egypt!'
- 'MY covenant!!'
- 'not obeyed ME!!'

As we've previously seen, and many, many theologians agree, the 'Angel of the Lord' appearances are 'Christophanies,' or appearances of Yeshua in the Tanak, AND, He is the One who brought them up from Egypt, swore to the Fathers and made the covenant . . . the ONE who demands obedience.

Just like at the end of the 'Jesus on Sinai' post, I sit here STUNNED! How has Christendom justified claiming that 'Jesus did away with the Law?' Or even, 'changed' or 'abrogated' any of it?

I am sorry, but that is absolute and utter fallacy!

James 4:12, Yeshua is the 'Lawgiver.'

He said in Matthew 5:18 that 'not the smallest letter or stroke will pass from the Law until all is accomplished.'

Hebrews 13:8, 'Yeshua the same yesterday, today and forever.'

Brothers and sisters, Yeshua (Jesus) is the atoning sacrifice that frees us from the curse of the Law and allows us back into covenant with Him! His covenant IS the Torah! He appeared to Moses in the burning bush to bring Israel OUT of Egypt. He calls us today to come out of Babylon! Leave the religious traditions behind and seek the TRUTH of the Word! Walk as He walked! If you love Him, keep HIS commandments, the Torah!

He saves us by His grace and calls us to obedience.

Please! Wake. UP.

Angel of the Lord Study Sheet

produced 7/19/15

The following are my notes for a Bible Study that I led on the topic of the Angel of the Lord. These notes are in bullet format because honestly, a book could be written on just these couple pages of notes. May they challenge and enrich your understanding of our Messiah and His relation to Yehovah and to us.

John 5:45-47 and Luke 24:27 – We should be able to see Yeshua in the Torah since "Moses wrote about Me."

Genesis 16:7-13 – Note the claims this 'malak' – messenger – makes:

- "I will multiply..."
- "Yehovah (The Lord) spoke with me..."
- "Have I remained alive after seeing Him?"

Read John 1:18 and 5:37. Who did Hagar see and hear that made these astounding claims?

Genesis 22:11-18 – Again, note the claims of the Angel of the Lord:

- "from Me..."
- "I will bless..."
- "My voice..."

Exodus 3:2-6 and following:

- "appeared..."
- "The Lord saw . . . God called from the midst"
- "holy ground." – worship
- "afraid to look at God"
- v.14: "I Am who I am"
- v.15: YHVH
- "to all generations"

[Aside: As previously mentioned, YHVH/Yahweh/Yehovah – name removed 6800 times from text. Check the translator notes in the front of your Bible... See Jeremiah 16:19-21]

Numbers 22:22-35
- v. 31: Angel of the Lord accepts worship (compare to other angels that say 'don't worship.')
- "contrary to <u>Me</u>"
- v. 35: "Speak only the words <u>I</u> tell you"
- Numbers 23:5: "Yehovah (The Lord) put a word in Balaam's mouth."

Exodus 14:19
- Angel of the Lord leads.
- Compare to Exodus 13:17-18 ("God did not lead, God led.")
- Compare Exodus 14:24 "Yehovah looked down . . . fire and smoke."

Judges 2:1-4 – Note again the astounding claims of the Angel of the Lord
- "<u>I</u> brought you out."
- "<u>I</u> have sworn to your fathers."
- "<u>My</u> Covenant."
- "have not obeyed <u>Me</u>!!"
- See Acts 7:38 "angel who was speaking with him on Mt. Sinai."

Judges 6:11-23
Note the claims:
- "Yehovah is with you..."
- "Have <u>I</u> not sent you?..."
- "<u>I</u> will be with you..."
- Accepts offering vss. 18, 20-21

Judges 13:2-23
- v. 3: "appeared"
- v.11: "I am..."
- v. 16 & 23: "burnt offering..."

- v. 18: "wonderful" (a riddle not understood for 500 years . . . compare Genesis 32:29-30 and Isaiah 9:6.)
- v.22: "We have seen God."

Deuteronomy 23:14 – Who walks in the midst of the camp?

Knowing all of this . . .

Exodus 24:9-11 – Remembering, 'no man can see God . . .'
- "they saw the God of Israel."
- "they saw God and He did not stretch out His hand."
- Who did they see?

The One they saw is the One Colossians 1:15 says is, "the image of the invisible God, the firstborn of all creation." The One they saw was Yeshua.

Knowing this, if Yeshua stood on Mt. Sinai, and James 4:12 calls Him the Lawgiver, and Hebrews 13:8 tells us [He is] "the same, yesterday, today, forever," then, what does He mean when He says, "If you love Me, you will keep MY commandments"?

What commandments is He talking about? What commandments did He give?

6 DOCTRINES OF MEN

Clearly, we can draw the conclusion that Yeshua was on Mt. Sinai. According to His own mouth, He can only teach the words of the Father. For that reason, we have to strongly re-evaluate Christian doctrines and dogma that claim parts of the everlasting Word are no longer valid or 'done away with.'

My journey toward more truth was clearly at odds with many doctrines I had been taught or had embraced through Christendom. While those who taught me meant the best and only taught what they had been taught, I could tell that some foundational material needed to be re-evaluated and, where appropriate, jettisoned.

Following are several articles holding my inherited doctrines against the truth of Scripture. There are dozens and dozens of similar articles at natsab.com. These are chosen to introduce you to various doctrinal topics that we need to explore further.

The Error of Dividing the Law

Originally posted on October 5, 2013.

For centuries, millennia, really, Christendom has embraced an error that is called the 'Three-Fold Division of the Law.' It is particularly prevalent in Reformed circles, sometimes even called a 'cornerstone' of reformed teaching. Most of the main streams of theology embrace the error to one degree or another as a means of justifying their particular theological bent.

The general gist of the position is that the Law of Moses can be divided into three categories: moral, civil, ceremonial; and that two of the three categories are no longer valid, or have been annulled/abrogated.

The thumbnail sketch of history will often assign the origins of this division to Thomas Aquinas in the 13th Century. Aquinas did articulate most clearly and popularize the system of thought, but the threads of this can be traced back to the mid-200s. (Those who desire a quick jaunt through history can read *The Threefold Division of the Law* by Jonathan F. Bayes. www.christian.org.uk/html-publications/theology/threefold.pdf. His conclusions are wrong as I will demonstrate, but his short article is a decent primer on the subject from The Christian Institute's perspective.)

John Calvin, in his *Institutes on the Christian Religion*, refers to the threefold division and thereby errantly lays the accepted foundation for much of Protestantism. Later, the *Westminster Confession of Faith* codified the division in chapter 19, paragraph 3:

> III. Besides this law, commonly called moral, God was pleased to give to the people of Israel, as a church under age, ceremonial laws, containing several typical ordinances, partly of worship, prefiguring Christ, His graces, actions, sufferings, and benefits; and partly,

holding forth divers instructions of moral duties. **All which ceremonial laws are now abrogated, under the New Testament.**

Just to be clear, 'abrogated,' according to Merriam-Webster's Dictionary means:

- to **abolish** by authoritative action: annul
- to treat as nonexistent <abrogating their responsibilities>

The threefold division is still much discussed and debated after 1700 years of church history have passed under the bridge. Not long ago, Philip Ross wrote a book about the divergent viewpoints within this debate. In his book, *From the Finger of God*, Ross defends the position, but admits that after all this time, even the wisest of the theologians cannot agree on where some laws fit and therefore the laws' applicability. Maybe that should be a hint that the whole idea has problems.

Instead of gathering opinion from man, let's see what Scripture has to say.

The obvious first place, and the insurmountable barrier to those who hold this position, are the words of the Lawgiver Himself;

Matthew 5:17-20
Do not think that I came to abolish the Law or the Prophets; I did not come to abolish but to fulfill. For truly I say to you, until heaven and earth pass away, not the smallest letter or stroke shall pass from the Law until all is accomplished. **Whoever then annuls one of the least of these commandments**, and teaches others to do the same, shall be called least in the kingdom of heaven; but whoever keeps and teaches them, he shall be called great in the kingdom of heaven. For I say to you that unless your righteousness surpasses that of the scribes and Pharisees, you will not enter the kingdom of heaven.

But that is not all Yeshua (Jesus) had to say...

Given the golden opportunity to divide the Law and/or set the stage for the 'dividing of the Law,' or abolishing thereof, see what He says:

Matthew 22:36-40

"Teacher, which is the great commandment in the Law?" And He said to him, "'You shall love the Lord your God with all your heart, and with all your soul, and with all your mind.' This is the great and foremost commandment. The second is like it, 'You shall love your neighbor as yourself.' **On these two commandments depend the <u>whole</u> Law and the Prophets.**" Matthew 22:36-40

Yeshua doesn't divide the law. Rather, He affirms the WHOLE of it by quoting Deuteronomy 6:5 and Leviticus 19:18. He affirms the indivisibility of it!!

In fact, Scripture NEVER divides the Law/Torah. Rather, it always speaks of it as a whole. Yes, Yeshua and others affirm that there are weightier matters of the Law, those that temporarily suspend others at certain points, but they do not nullify, annul, abolish or abrogate anything. (An example would be the 'work' of circumcising a boy on the eighth day if it fell on a Sabbath. The Sabbath 'no work' law is temporarily suspended for the weightier law of circumcision.)

Without belaboring the point, suffice it to say, Torah will be written on our heart in the 'new' covenant:

Jeremiah 31:33

"But this is the covenant which I will make with the house of Israel after those days," declares the Lord, "**I will put My law (Torah) within them and on their heart I will write it**; and I will be their God, and they shall be My people." (See Jeremiah 31:31-34 for larger context.)

So, how did theologians get to the place where they divided the Law? And why?

I will speculate a little here, so bear with me.

I think there are two major contributing factors to why the Law was divided.

First, increasing anti-Semitism by the Roman empire from the middle first century on fostered a climate where the new Gentile believers sought, errantly, to separate themselves from anything that looked 'Jewish.' Thus, reasoning was needed to avoid those things Scripture says 'set you apart,' like feasts, diet, day of worship and dress. I wrote previously about how Scripture defines these very things as marks of holiness, or set-apartness. [Lest I be misunderstood, let me be abundantly clear: **Works do NOT save**. We are saved by faith in the blood of Messiah Yeshua. <u>Good works are the evidence</u> that we have entered, by His blood, into covenant with Him!]

So, those who sought to redefine believers in Yeshua into a new religion did so by redefining some of the commandments of Yahweh as 'Jewish,' and then distancing themselves from them through warped theology. This was confirmed by an astute political move by Constantine that proves, even in 325 CE, many believers in Messiah were still celebrating the feasts, worshiping on the Sabbath, and eating foods the Bible defines as clean (Lev. 11). The Bishops of Rome, being his co-conspirators, affirmed his ruling through their theology, setting the course even for those who 'protest' their mother, the Roman Catholic Church.'

Secondly, the destruction of the Temple in Jerusalem, as well as the diaspora of the Jews, became a major challenge to theological thought concerning those laws deemed 'ceremonial' and 'civil.' Instead of rightly understanding these to be 'suspended,' as the Jews did when they went into captivity to Babylon, they assumed them abolished or annulled at the cross of Yeshua.

To take this position, theologians have to ignore numerous verses that point to Rav Shaul (Paul) keeping the feasts and offering sacrifices. They have to ignore verses in Hebrews, written decades after the resurrection of Messiah, that state the offerings were being offered 'according to the law' at the time of writing. They have to countermand the very words of Messiah when He says, 'until heaven and earth pass away . . . not one jot or tittle will pass from the Law...' Ouch!

Without going into great detail, dividing the Law creates more problems than it 'solves.'

As previously demonstrated, dividing the Law is directly contrary to the testimony of Scripture about it being 'holy,' 'just,' good,' etc. Further, it is opposed to the words of Messiah, the Lawgiver, particularly when He says,

John 14:15
If you love Me, you will keep My commandments.

and,

John 7:16
What I teach doesn't come from me but from the one who sent me.

Perhaps the most glaring non-Scriptural evidence is the fact that once we accept the idea that the Law can be divided, it opens the door for anyone to divide it according to their own proclivities. Just reference the book by Ross, then, go read how some of the more liberal denominations are defining sins that the Torah calls 'abominations.'

Another problem with dividing the Torah is that Christianity makes itself into a hypocrite by preaching that the ceremonial laws are abrogated, but then they pass the offering plate requesting your tithe according to the commandments of that same ceremonial law. Hmmmm.

Still another glaring problem is the clear reference to 'ceremonial laws' in passages of Scripture that theologians almost universally call 'millennial.' Consider Isaiah 66:16-24 or Zechariah 14:16-21 for future prophecy on food (e.g., not eating swine), Sabbaths, new moon festivals, Feast of Booths (Tabernacles), sacrifices at the Temple, and a priesthood. Reformed Presbyterians (and many other denominational groups) dodge this bullet by declaring that there is no such thing as a 'millennial reign,' contrary to Revelation 20:1-7. The result is to spiritualize and warp, or altogether ignore, a HUGE pile of prophetic passages.

These problems alone should be enough to give cause for concern about dividing the Law.

Part of the defense for the Threefold Error is expressed by Jonathan Bayes in his previously mentioned article. Scriptures expressing Yahweh's displeasure with sacrifices are paraded out in classic 'proof-texting' form. The context from which the passages come is ignored, as is the larger context of Scripture previously generalized. See Bayes' citations and then read in context to find that the Father's desire is not the termination of sacrifice and offering, but rather, Yahweh desires a contrite heart so that the sacrifice and offering is accepted!

Bayes' use of these verses, evidencing the wicked hearts of those offering sacrifices, is to demonstrate that the sacrifices are useless and thus voidable. He ignores verses that say,

Isaiah 42:21-22
The Lord was pleased for His righteousness' sake to make the law (Torah) great and glorious. But this is a people plundered and despoiled; all of them are trapped in caves, or are hidden away in prisons; they have become a prey with none to deliver them, and a spoil, with none to say, "Give them back!"

The problem isn't the Torah!! The problem is the people!!

This same false dichotomy is used by those who try to prove the Torah has been done away with by citing passages such as this one from Hebrews:

Hebrews 8:8
For finding fault **with them**, He says, "Behold, days are coming, says the Lord, when I will effect a new covenant with the house of Israel and with the house of Judah;

In their bias, theologians read this verse and see 'for finding fault with IT' (meaning Torah), but the text says, 'THEM' (meaning the people of Israel to whom the Torah was given). The problem is not and never has been the Torah. The problem is the heart of man.

Abolishing and rejecting two thirds of the Torah does not make man more righteous or give him an easier path to righteousness! A circumcised heart is what leads to righteousness!

God's Word has not failed, nor does He need a 'plan B.'

The Torah still stands! It is the everlasting covenant! Messiah simply opens a way for us to be grafted into His rich root and become a member of the commonwealth of Israel.

Of course, those who divide the Law get to this point and decide to try using absurd twists on the Torah to make points. They say, 'Oh, so you won't mix threads? See how that flies at Walmart!' Or, 'I guess you are sacrificing in your backyard?' Or, 'Gonna stone your children? That's what Torah says to do to your rebellious children!'

These sorts of obnoxious absurdities reveal two things:

First, and foremost, getting these types of comments, particularly from pastors and those trained in theology, is deeply troubling. Many, many of these types of comments reveal a profound lack of understanding and knowledge of the Torah and what it actually teaches. As a seminary trained former pastor, I can honestly tell you, the vast majority of those with seminary training and degrees have NO real understanding of Torah and have so many anti-Semitic presuppositional biases to deal with that it is hard to even have intelligent discourse.

Most prefer ignorance, despite the fact that as an excuse it will be of no value before the Creator when they have to give account. (If you are a pastor reading this, instead of getting huffy, I would recommend taking off your denominational filters/glasses, and prayerfully asking the King to reveal TRUTH to you! Dare to ask Him to reveal any anti-Semitism or falsehood in your thought process. Be a man and buck up! -I can say that! I walked in your shoes.)

Secondly, these obnoxious absurdities reveal a heart condition. Basically, there are two types of believers: Those who look for ways to fulfill the commands as best they can according to the Torah, and those who look for ways around the commands, despite clear Scriptural evidence to the contrary. The first demonstrates a circumcised heart, while the second is evidence of a stiff-neck. Which are you? Do you prayerfully seek to do all that you can do, leaving the rest for the Father to take care of? Or, do you search the Scriptures for proof-text verses that support your desire to avoid obedience?

Instead of committing the error of dividing the Law and looking to justify ways around it like our fathers did, should we not be seeking to do all that God asks of those who love Him, while leaving the details, or 'impossible' ones up to Him?

I choose to obey and walk as closely as I can, trusting that He can work out the details where I may not understand it all, until He comes again to teach rightly His Torah.

Abba, I pray for myself and these, my readers. Open our eyes and give us hearts that simply desire to be obedient to your Word. Give us understanding and clarity as we seek truth. Show us how to love You in the ways You ask to be loved. Please do so for Your Name's sake!! Amein!

Of elephants and theologians

Originally posted on October 1, 2013.

On an unnamed blog that I read from time to time, the question was asked,

> We understand that the Old Covenant was inaugurated with blood (Ex. 34) and its terms were verbally established for God's people through the giving of the Law. If the New Covenant was similarly inaugurated with blood (Luke 22), when was its content verbally established?

As soon as I saw the question, fireworks went off in my head! Here is an Achilles heel!

Because that blog is largely frequented by Reformed pastors and elders, I chose to watch it for 24 hours before responding. I wanted to see what answers would be posted by a 'covenantal theology' crowd.

Frankly, I was deeply disappointed. I shouldn't have been, because a simple look at the question reveals that it can only lead where Christendom does NOT want to go, thus revealing an Achilles heel.

What indeed ARE the terms of the 'New' Covenant? Where are they stated? Is it a mystery we have to tease out of the text or is our God One who reveals His expectations clearly and plainly?

Honestly, the question hung in the air and only a few responded in the first 24 hours with some not even understanding the question and no consensus among the others.

It is a simple question, really. Maybe one we need to ask of the learned more often. They have no consensus and no real answer, thus revealing that, either,

1. We are expected by Yahweh to figure out what the terms are from the various saying of Yeshua and Rav Shaul (Paul), or

2. We HAVE the terms of the covenant clearly articulated in the Torah and indeed it is a <u>renewed</u> covenant.

They do not want to go to #2 at ANY cost, because it exposes multiple holes in Christian theology, so they take wild stabs, all the while ignoring the elephant in the room.

When I could stand it no longer, 24 hours being about my limit, I posted this response:

You ask a fascinating question.

Jesus said, "My doctrine is not mine, but his that sent me." Jn 7:16 KJV

The Father, through the author of Proverbs (4:2, KJV) says, "For I give you good doctrine, forsake ye not my law (torah)."

At the end of the Sermon on the Mount we read, "And it came to pass, when Jesus had ended these sayings, the people were astonished at his doctrine:" Matthew 7:28 KJV. (He didn't teach anything new. He simply expanded to the heart what was generally practiced as an outward work.)

What was Jesus speaking ? The Father, through Moses in Deuteronomy 18:18 (NASB) says, "I will raise up a prophet from among their countrymen like you, and I will put My words in His mouth and he shall speak to them all that I command him."

Read Deuteronomy 13:1-5. Jesus, like all true prophets, could not teach anything that even sniffed of departing from the commandments. See v. 4! And, He did say, "I did not come to abolish the law . . . until heaven and earth pass away. . . ." Matthew 5:17-19

Scripture teaches that Jesus will return and reign from Mt. Zion.

Isaiah 2:1-5 . . . v. 2 "it will come about in the last days. . . ." v. 3b says, "For the law (torah) will go forth from Zion, and the word of the Lord from Jerusalem."

But that makes sense because James referred to Jesus as "the Lawgiver and Judge." (4:12) (Even some Jewish sages/rabbis believe the Messiah was on Mt. Sinai at the giving of the Law! Pg 64 of Return of the Kosher Pig *by Rabbi Itzhak Shapira quoting ancient sources as he, a Messianic believer in Yeshua, makes the case for a Divine Messiah from Rabbinic writings. Fascinating scholarly book to see the battle for Yeshua from the other side!! http://www.kosherpig.org or his Youtube videos. But, I digress.)*

So, what is this 'new' thing? (Your question)

The Father says, "Surely the Lord God does nothing unless He reveals His secret counsel to His servants the prophets." Amos 3:7 (NASB)

So, what exactly did He reveal to Jeremiah in 31:31-34?

1. 'new' covenant. The Hebrew word for 'new' means 'refresh, renew, restore' etc. according to the Ancient Hebrew Lexicon. i.e., the covenant that Israel had broken and been scattered as a result of breaking, would be renewed opening the door for all who come, to be grafted in through the blood of Messiah.

2. The 'new' covenant is with the House of Israel and the House of Judah. This is a tough pill for Christendom to swallow, because we've been taught our whole lives that the covenant is with us. The reality is, we are grafted into Israel through the blood of Messiah! See Ephesians 2. The whole chapter, but particularly v. 12. We become members of the commonwealth of Israel. What does 'adoption/grafting in' really mean? Different rules? Different system? Different treatment? How then do we become 'one new man?'

3. The law (torah) will be put in their/our hearts. When Jeremiah wrote this, do we honestly think he believed a new law would be given when the first was called 'perfect,' 'holy,' righteous,' etc.?

Jeremiah goes on to reveal how sure this is in 33:14-22. Notice 'covenant,' 'house of Judah,' house of Israel,' 'David,' 'My servant,' 'heaven,' 'earth,' and 'Levitical priests.' God affirms that He WILL do this.

We've been taught that the 'Law of Moses' is BAD!

Scripture says, 'How blessed are those whose way is blameless, who walk in the law (torah) of the Lord.' And, 'in keeping them there is great reward.' And, 'I love your law (torah)' And, 'If you love Me, you will keep My commandments' (covenant loyalty language...) etc., etc.

We've been taught that the Law of Moses is 'too hard.'

Scripture says, "For this commandment which I command you today is not too difficult for you, nor is it out of reach."

We've been taught that the Law of Moses is done away with.

Scripture says, "Do we then nullify the Law through faith? May it never be! On the contrary, we establish the Law" and "until heaven and earth pass away, not one jot or tittle will pass from the Law."

[Ma'am], the terms of the covenant have been written down and are well established. Unfortunately, those terms are the 'elephant in the room.' Christendom has to begin to deal with why they allowed Paul to be twisted to say things he never said (2 Peter 3:14-17), and why we allowed pagan syncretism in the door

through Constantine and many of the early church 'fathers.'

I could write much more...

Shalom.

Shortly after that reply, I was asked to take a seat as my thoughts were not what the author was looking for. I got a bowl of popcorn and sat to observe them continue to fumble for an answer to the question, 'What are the terms of the New Covenant?'

Indeed, there is an elephant in the room.

Westminster Confession Errors

Originally posted on July 25, 2015.

The many posts I have written concerning doctrines of men include several series. This post is the first in a series dealing with doctrinal error in the Westminster Confession of Faith.

As a young boy and through my teen years, I was reared in a church that was part of the Presbyterian Church in America (PCA) denomination. The actual congregation my family was a part of, Lebanon Presbyterian Church, was founded in 1775 and had Scots Irish roots that connected her to a system of doctrine often termed 'Reformed.' Today, many Presbyterian denominations have drifted into gross liberalism, but the PCA has remained fairly 'conservative' as the descriptor goes.

With the rich history and proud heritage of the Scots Irish Presbyterians, I was taught that the best and only reasonable understanding of Scripture was based on the Westminster Confession of Faith, a doctrinal statement forged by the Assembly of Divines at Westminster Abbey in England between 1643 and 1647. To question or disagree with that document was tantamount to heresy. It is regarded as THE proper distillation of Scripture, and departure from it potentially endangers the soul.

In my early 30s, the Father reigned in my Jonah trip through the military and the business world, bringing me to seminary and eventually a pastoral position in the Associate Reformed Presbyterian Church, another Scots Irish denomination with a long and storied history that adheres to the Westminster Confession of Faith (WCF). My own denomination viewed my seminary credentials with some distrust, as they did for most any candidate who attended a seminary that was not 'confessional.' I attended a very conservative seminary that had students and professors from a very broad base of doctrinal positions, but the exposure to other thought processes was considered to be potentially problematic. While my peers would disagree with my assessment, the questioning of belief structure is always more intense around pastoral candidates who ventured outside the chosen lines of 'doctrinal purity.'

While I could go into much more detail with this explanation and give multiple examples, I offer this much to say,

Within Reformed denominations, Scripture is read through the filter of the Westminster Confession of Faith. More precisely, the Westminster Confession of Faith is a man-made document that governs the Reformed understanding of Scripture and thereby is held as a judge over the Word of God.

My intent is to demonstrate clearly that some parts of the WCF are grossly out of line with the clear Word of my King. By doing so, I hope that the readers will question whatever doctrinal statement they may have bought into in order to identify areas of error that are not in accordance with Scripture.

Like most doctrinal statements, there is much good in the WCF. However, it only takes a few errors to radically alter a system of thought such that it appears to be truth while in fact it codifies and perpetuates falsehood. At times, that falsehood can have eternal consequences, and yes, I dared say that! Beware using the traditions of men to filter the Word of God!!

I want us to look at Chapter XIX (19) of the WCF. This chapter, titled "Of the Law of God", contains 7 paragraphs which we will consider in turn. I will not exhaustively disassemble; my intent is only to clearly demonstrate that when held to the light of Scripture, the Westminster Confession of Faith does not hold water as tightly as I was taught. [Note: I have left in the Scripture proofs annotations so that the reader can see that each statement is in one way or another supported by some Scripture, though careful study reveals that the full counsel of Scripture is often not taken into account, or the verse used is taken out of context.]

> *I. God gave to Adam a law, as a covenant of works, by which He bound him and all his posterity, to personal,*

entire, exact, and perpetual obedience, promised life upon the fulfilling, and threatened death upon the breach of it, and endued him with power and ability to keep it.[1]

Here begins a solid paragraph with which I do not have any major issue.

*II. This law, after his fall, **continued to be a perfect rule of righteousness**; and, as such, was delivered by God upon Mount Sinai, in ten commandments, and written in two tables[2]: the first four commandments containing our duty towards God; and the other six, our duty to man.*[3]

In bold we have our first curious statement. 'This law . . . continued to be a perfect rule of righteousness.' Read this very slowly and comprehend: 'perfect rule of righteousness.'

Scripture indeed teaches that this law is THE perfect rule of righteousness, not 'a perfect rule of righteousness.' As we continue through the WCF's commentary on 'the Law of God,' we will see that like most of Christendom, they may say it is a 'perfect rule of righteousness,' but they deny its authority or the standard of righteousness it teaches by diminishing it. Further, its perfection is obviously undermined by the denial that it is currently the standard of God and in the future will be the standard of God as taught by the Messiah from Zion. Isaiah 2:1-5 clearly teaches that 'in the last days,' the nations will stream to Zion so that 'He may teach us concerning His ways, and that we may walk in His paths, for **the Torah will go forth from Zion** and the word of the Lord from Jerusalem.'

III. Besides this law, commonly called moral, God was pleased to give to the people of Israel, as a church under age, ceremonial laws, containing several typical ordinances, partly of worship, prefiguring Christ, His graces, actions, sufferings, and benefits;[4] and partly, holding forth divers instructions of moral duties.[5] All which ceremonial laws are now abrogated, under the New Testament.[6]

Even a casual reading of this paragraph exposes multiple errors that are brazen contradictions of Scripture.

Our first is the use of the phrase 'commonly called moral,' followed by a seemingly intelligent statement beginning with 'ceremonial laws.' Understand, the idea of a division in God's instructions (Torah) into 'moral, ceremonial and judicial' categories that can then be treated differently is entirely a man-made construct that is contrary to Scripture. God does not EVER in His instructions even remotely allude to the system Roman Catholic Christendom commonly calls the Three-fold Division of the Law. I have written about this error multiple times. In descending order of relevance, here are three articles: "The Error of Dividing the Law", "Leviticus 19 ~ Apologetically, A Most Useful Chapter!", and "Protestant Hypocrisy?". Search them at natsab.com.

Second, as part of the 'ceremonial' laws that are 'abrogated,' the WCF lists 'several typical ordinances.' Well, it would seem the Westminster Divines did not read closely verses like Exodus 12:14 and 24, that say, "So this day shall be to you a memorial; and you shall keep it as a feast to the Lord **throughout your generations**. You shall keep it as a feast by an **everlasting ordinance**," and "you shall observe this thing as an ordinance for you and your sons **forever**." Christendom often plays with the definition of 'forever,' but they can't argue with Malachi 4:4-6 that clearly states that in the last days (before the Day of the Lord) we need to 'remember the Torah of Moses, even the statutes and the ordinances.' Folks, this is no small error. But, let's continue.

Third, this paragraph having multiple gargantuan errors, we have to consider the phrase 'all which ceremonial laws are now abrogated.' This sentence is stunning in its clear violation of a number of Scriptures. Besides the multiple places we are expressly told of 'ceremonial laws' being adhered to in the

Millennial Kingdom [see Ezekiel 43-44 (esp. 43:18ff); Zechariah 14:16-21; and Isaiah 66:22-23], Yeshua (Jesus) Himself said, "Do not think that I came to abolish the Law or the Prophets; I did not come to abolish but to fulfill..." [FYI: 'Abolish' and 'abrogate' mean the same thing. See Merriam-Webster.] Yeshua says, 'I did NOT come to abolish,' but the WCF says, 'all which are abrogated (abolished).' Guess who I believe?!!

There are more problems with this paragraph, but those three sufficiently put the kibosh on the whole chapter!! We'll move on.

> *IV. To them also, as a body politic, He gave sundry judicial laws, which expired together with the State of that people; not obliging under any now, further than the general equity thereof may require.*[7]

There are several issues with this short paragraph, chief of which is the assertion that the 'State of that people' has 'expired.' True, at the time of the writing of the WCF, the authors could hardly imagine a day wherein Israel would again exist as a nation, but even a simple reading of the Scripture in multiple places demonstrates that Israel proper will exist until heaven and earth pass away. Jeremiah 31:35-37 is one example. But the further idea that the 'judicial laws' have expired stands false on several counts. First, see the 'everlasting' nature of God's Law and the previously mentioned fallacy of dividing the Law into categories that can then be kept or 'abrogated.' Second, some of the parameters necessary for the employment of God's Law may not currently be in place (i.e., Temple, Levitical Priesthood, Sanhedrin, etc.), but that in no way nullifies the Laws. It merely suspends them until the proper conditions again exist. And, Scripture promises that those conditions will again exist and the Laws will rightly be employed by the Messiah Himself. (See Isaiah 2:3-4; Psalm 2:7-12; Micah 4:2-3; etc.)

> *V. The moral law does forever bind all, as well justified persons as others, to the obedience thereof;*[8] *and that,*

not only in regard of the matter contained in it, but also in respect of the authority of God the Creator, who gave it.[9] *Neither does Christ, in the Gospel, any way dissolve, but much strengthen this obligation.*[10]

Here, very neatly, the WCF affirms that Yeshua does not 'dissolve, but much strengthens the obligation' of the 'moral law,' but by its absence, the Divines undermine the 'ceremonial' and 'judicial' portions of their divisions of the Law. Like the moral law that forever binds, Scripture previously presented declares that the rest of the law also forever binds, contrary to the WCF implication.

VI. Although true believers be not under the law, as a covenant of works, to be thereby justified, or condemned;[11] *yet is it of great use to them, as well as to others; in that, as a rule of life informing them of the will of God, and their duty, it directs and binds them to walk accordingly;*[12] *discovering also the sinful pollutions of their nature, hearts and lives;*[13] *so as, examining themselves thereby, they may come to further conviction of, humiliation for, and hatred against sin,*[14] *together with a clearer sight of the need they have of Christ, and the perfection of His obedience.*[15] *It is likewise of use to the regenerate, to restrain their corruptions, in that it forbids sin:*[16] *and the threatenings of it serve to show what even their sins deserve; and what afflictions, in this life, they may expect for them, although freed from the curse thereof threatened in the law.*[17] *The promises of it, in like manner, show them God's approbation of obedience, and what blessings they may expect upon the performance thereof:*[18] *although not as due to them by the law as a covenant of works.*[19] *So as, a man's doing good, and refraining from evil, because the law encourages to the one and deters from the other, is no evidence of his being under the law: and not under grace.*[20]

While this paragraph is largely correct in its wording and phrasing, neither the Westminster Divines nor present Reformed Presbyterians believe it according to how it reads.

Scripture uses the phrase 'under the law' (hupo nomon) eleven times. JK McKee's scholarly book, *The New Testament Validates Torah*, demonstrates that the only consistent and reasonable understanding of this phrase in Scripture is 'under the condemnation of the law.' Ironically, that is exactly how the phrase should be understood in the above paragraph. However, the Divines intend the phrase in the commonly misused meaning that is pandemic in Christendom: we are not subject to the Law and it has no authority over us. Yet, in the very next lines they affirm that the law is 'the will of God,' defines sin, leads to Messiah, etc. Essentially, they see the Law as something to which they need only give mental assent while ignoring the actual doing of major parts of it.

Truly, we are not under the condemnation of the law. However, we are still responsible to it as the will of God, as a guide for sanctified living, as a definer and identifier of sin, as the only standard of righteousness, etc. All of those require that we 'walk' in obedience even as our Messiah did.

The last sentence is particularly amusing in that it is starkly contrasted by the actual actions of most of Christendom, never mind adherents to the WCF. The sentence says,

> So as, a man's doing good, and refraining from evil, because the law encourages to the one and deters from the other, is no evidence of his being under the law: and not under grace.

Over and over, from Christians of all stripes, I have been told that if I keep the Law, I place myself at risk of 'losing my salvation' because the immediate and false assumption is that I am trying to earn my salvation by works. Utterly absurd. Yet, I've heard the very fallacious line from friends, family and Reformed Presbyterian pastors whose own document states that 'doing good . . . because the law encourages [it] . . . is NO evidence of being under the [condemnation] of the law. . . .' Amazing.

> *VII. Neither are the forementioned uses of the law contrary to the grace of the Gospel, but do sweetly comply with it;[21] the Spirit of Christ subduing and enabling the will of man to do that freely, and cheerfully, which the will of God, revealed in the law, requires to be done.[22]*

In this last paragraph, I again see no error. However, the Reformers' definition of what is the Law does not square with what Scripture says is the Law. As we have previously seen, the WCF sees the 'ceremonial' and 'civil' or 'judicial' aspects of the Law have been abrogated/abolished and therefore are not included in their definition of 'Law.' Conversely, the Torah, all of it, every jot and tittle according to Yeshua, applies until heaven and earth pass away.

The Reformers rightly understand that the law 'reveals the will of God' and is what is 'required to be done.' In that, they are again correct, but because they have a skewed view of what the Law actually is, their understanding and adherence, or non-adherence, is, by definition, wrong.

As we have seen, Chapter XIX of the Westminster Confession of Faith both contains errors when held next to Scripture, and in some areas that are rightly stated, we find wrong implementation of understanding. Some readers may take comfort that they do not follow the WCF. Beware, however; most other Christian doctrinal systems have similar errors in their understanding and adherence to the Law of God (Torah of Moses). Anytime we use the traditions or doctrines of men to filter Scripture, we place them in judgment over the Word of God and allow them to be our judge of the Most High!

Beware the traditions of men!

Additional parts of this series are at natsab.com.

---

1 - Gen. 1:26-27; 2:17; Rom. 2:14-15; 10:5; 5:12, 19; Gal. 3:10, 12; Eccl. 7:29; Job 28:28

2 – Jam. 1:25; 2:8, 10-12; Ro,. 13:8-9; Deu.5:32; 10:4; Ex. 34:1

3 – Matt. 22:37-40

4 – Heb. 9; 10:1; Gal. 4:1-3; Col. 2:17

5 – 1 Cor. 5:7; 2 Cor. 6:17; Jude 23

6 – Col. 2:14, 16, 17; Dan. 9:27; Eph. 2:15-16

7 – Ex. 21; 22:1-29; Gen. 49:10; 1 Pe. 2:13-14; Matt. 5:17, 38-39; 1 Cor. 9:8-10

8 – Rom.13:8, 9; Eph. 6:2; 1 John 2:3-4, 7-8

9 – Jam. 2:10, 11

10 - Matt. 5:17-19; Jam. 2:8; Rom. 3:31

11 – Rom. 6:14; Gal. 2:16; 3:13; 4:4-5; Acts 13:39; Rom. 8:1

12 – Rom. 7:12, 22, 25; Ps. 119:4-6; 1 cor. 7:19; Gal. 5:14, 16, 18-23

13 – Rom. 7:7; 3:20

14 – Jam. 1:23-25; Rom. 7:9, 14, 24

15 – Gal. 3:24; Rom. 7:24; 8:3-4

16 – Jam. 2:11; Ps. 119:101, 104, 128

17 – Ezra 9:13-14; Ps. 84:30-34

18 – Lev. 26:1-14; 2 Cor. 6:16; Eph. 6:2-3; Ps. 37:11; Matt. 5:5; Ps. 19:11

19 – Gal. 2:16; Luke 17:10

20 – Rom. 6:12, 14; 1 Pe. 3:8-12; Ps. 34:12-16; Heb. 12:28-29

21 – Gal. 3:21

22 – Ezek. 36:27; Heb. 8:10; Jer. 31:33

7 IT IS ALL ABOUT THE KINGDOM

In Christendom, we are taught a great deal about personal salvation and the personal redemptive work of Yeshua. We live and breathe the grace He shed on us in saving us from our sins and our future hope of Heaven, but do we ever stop and really consider that His mission, His ministry was not focused on personal salvation and redemption? Sure, that is a part of His ministry, because we need personal redemption, but *why* do we need to be redeemed?

His primary purpose was to begin the process of restoring His people to their covenant calling, obedience to the 'rules of the House,' and the restoration of the Kingdom of Israel. Truly, a major portion of His purpose from His own Words as well as from the testimony of the prophets is the ultimate fulfillment of the plan God had from the beginning! YHVH's plan was a people, a nation, that displayed His glory throughout Creation as He brought restoration to the world through them.

Indeed, *the Torah was a national Constitution*, a very simple set of rules by which a people could relate with God, each other and the rest of the world. He purposed to make the Torah great and glorious (Isaiah 42:21), and to have His King on the throne of David ruling and reigning in righteousness (Isaiah 2:1-5).

God has no 'Plan B.' All of history, even today, is steadily moving toward the great culmination wherein the reconstituted people of Israel live in the Greater Israel promised to Abraham and his descendants under the reign of Yeshua, Messiah ben David.

We have considered Torah, the rule of that Kingdom. Here are a couple thoughts on the restoration of that kingdom.

Acts 1:6-7 – Yeshua on the Kingdom of Israel

Originally posted on March 19, 2014.

If you were to receive the very bad news that you only had 40 days to live, how would you spend those days? Who would you spend them with? What would you talk about? Is it safe to say that you would make the very most of those days relaying everything you could of importance to those following in your footsteps, be they children or whoever was taking your place at work. Wouldn't your conversations be focused on important matters and transmitting vital information?

After His resurrection, Yeshua had 40 final days with His disciples. I am certain that the conversations between them during that time contained deeply instructive revelations from the Scripture. (Recall, the only Scripture they had was the Tanak, the 'Old Testament!') He knew that He was leaving and would be gone for a while.

We are not told the content of those interactions, but we can take a few hints from the 'Road to Emmaus' conversation (Luke 24:13-35) and several other passages. One such passage is the very final conversation Yeshua had with His disciples. Let's read and consider,

Acts 1:6-7
So when they had come together, they were asking Him, saying, "Lord, is it at this time You are restoring the kingdom to Israel?" He said to them, "It is not for you to know times or epochs which the Father has fixed by His own authority. . . ."

Christendom has long held that everything changed at the cross. They believe that to one degree or another, from that point forward, Israel as a nation was no longer relevant, or of little relevance. Many denominations teach the replacement of the Jews by the new 'Israel of God.' By teaching these errors,

Christendom makes the disciples and Yeshua appear to be incredibly dumb and/or incompetent.

The disciples have been with Yeshua as his talmidim (disciples), learning from Him day and night for quite a while. Estimates vary from 70 weeks to upwards of 180 weeks! Yeshua the Messiah has been teaching and preparing them to take His message to all nations! Now, they ask their final question: 'Adonai, is it at this time You are restoring the kingdom to Israel?'

This is HUGE!!

After all this time walking in the dust of the Master, breaking bread, late night chats, miles and miles of roads, etc., they expect Him to restore the kingdom to Israel!! Either the disciples have monumentally missed everything He was teaching, OR Christendom has monumentally misunderstood the Messiah's mission.

We should hold our collective breath for His answer. Does He chastise them for misunderstanding all He has taught them? Does He chide them for being so Israel-centric? Or, does He simply say, 'It is not for you to know the times or seasons,' implying that the question is the correct one, but they do not need the answer right now.

Christianity often acts as if the disciples were not real bright and couldn't figure out the Messiah's purpose, which, whether they admit it or not, reflects poorly on the One who chose and trained the twelve. Yeshua doesn't respond to the disciples' question about restoring the kingdom as if they have missed a key point. He makes NO insinuation that they didn't 'get it.'

Rather, the very nature of Yeshua's answer indicates that indeed He plans to restore the kingdom to Israel, just 'not at this time.' Surely James understands, because in Acts 15 he points to a 'restored tent of David' that includes the grafted in Gentiles. Peter later writes to the 'scattered aliens' who 'were continually straying like sheep but have now returned to the Shepherd and Guardian of their souls.'

These dear men understood that the prophecies of a restored kingdom over which the Good Shepherd would rule would be fulfilled in a literal way! Even in His last conversation, just before He parts from them, Yeshua affirms a restoration of Israel, not a replacement!!

Read again, slowly, this short exchange and notice what is said and what is NOT said!!

Acts 1:5-7
So when they had come together, they were asking Him, saying, "Lord, is it at this time You are restoring the kingdom to Israel?" He said to them, "It is not for you to know times or epochs which the Father has fixed by His own authority. . . ."

As I read and pondered this passage again, something else about it stands out to me . . . the phrase, 'times or epochs.'

Did you know there are only two verses in the New Testament that have both of these words in them? Acts 1:7 is the first. The second is highly significant: 1 Thessalonians 5:1! Here it is in context:

I Thessalonians 5:1-4
Now as to the **times and the epochs**, brethren, you have no need of anything to be written to you. For you yourselves know full well that the day of the Lord will come just like a thief in the night. While they are saying, "Peace and safety!" then destruction will come upon them suddenly like labor pains upon a woman with child, and they will not escape. But you, brethren, are not in darkness, that the day would overtake you like a thief;

Notice a couple things:
- 'times and epochs' is associated with 'the Day of the Lord.'

- 'They' (unbelieving/unaware) are juxtaposed with 'but you' who are in the light (metaphor for Torah).
- Larger context dealing with the timing of the coming of Messiah points directly to the 'moedim,' the set times/Feasts of Yahweh! (See Gen. 1:14, Lev. 23)

In Acts 1, Yeshua not only does NOT correct the disciples' understanding of the restoration of the kingdom TO Israel, but gives a veiled pointer to WHEN this will happen. As we see from the word connection to 1 Thessalonians 5:1-4, the full restoration of Kingdom Israel will happen at 'the Day of the Lord,' the time of His return. The apostle Paul affirms this understanding and common ground with the disciples in Ephesians 2 when he speaks of the 'strangers and aliens' being grafted INTO the commonwealth of Israel and no longer being strangers to the covenants of promise! Paul further demonstrates this same understanding by quoting from Hosea and Isaiah in Romans 9-11. In one passage he specifically uses a passage from Hosea directed at the dispersed Northern Kingdom, or 'house of Israel.'

Romans 9:25-26

As He says also in Hosea, "I will call those who were not My people, 'My people,' and her who was not beloved, 'beloved.' And it shall be that in the place where it was said to them, 'you are not My people,' there they shall be called sons of the living God."

Beware those who teach that the church IS Israel or has somehow 'replaced' Israel. Those who teach such are not accurately reflecting the whole counsel of God's Word. Also, beware those who teach that the church escapes some tribulation reserved just for the Jews. This is another teaching that simply does not line up with the whole testimony of Scripture.

Rather, ponder these verses and the many, many others that point to the coming King who will restore, rebuild, and replant Israel.

Shalom!

Excellent passage defending Messianic Torah observance!!

Originally posted on December 28, 2013.

Here is an interesting passage that I already knew was a solid defense for Torah observance by the believer in Yeshua, but, while referring to it in a Shabbat message, I noticed a couple words that have been there all along! Funny how we can read verses and not SEE what is actually there.

Before we look at it, I want you to notice this is a 'last days' passage. Verse two gets quoted with the coming of Yeshua, but most never notice the context is decidedly eschatological. End times! Last days! Has 'not yet happened!!'

Malachi 4:1-6

"For behold, the day is coming, burning like a furnace; and all the arrogant and every evildoer will be chaff; and the day that is coming will set them ablaze," says the Lord of hosts, "so that it will leave them neither root nor branch. But for you who fear My name, the sun of righteousness will rise with healing in its wings; and you will go forth and skip about like calves from the stall. You will tread down the wicked, for they will be ashes under the soles of your feet on the day which I am preparing," says the Lord of hosts.
"Remember the TORAH of Moses My servant, even the statutes and ordinances which I commanded him in Horeb for all Israel. Behold, I am going to send you Elijah the prophet **before the coming of the great and terrible day of the Lord.** He will restore the hearts of the fathers to their children and the hearts of the children to their fathers, so that I will not come and smite the land with a curse."

Did you see that? Verse 4!! 'even the statutes and ordinances.'

Christendom tries to redefine what 'the Law of Moses' is that we are required to keep. Tradition ignores the Sabbath, feasts of the Lord and the clean/unclean food laws.

But here, in the last chapter of the last book of the Old Testament, is a passage that clearly speaks to a time yet future, and it instructs us to '**Remember the Torah of Moses, even the statutes and ordinances.**'

Our Father's Word is so simple. Frankly, at times, my seminary education is more of a hindrance than a help. His instructions are clearly written on every page. Only theological gymnastics and somersaults can take a simple passage like this and change its meaning!

Ponder!

8 BUT, BUT, BUT . . . WHAT ABOUT PAUL??

The discussion of the place of God's Instructions in Righteousness, His Torah, always leads back to Paul because so much Christian doctrine is based on his New Testament letters. Unfortunately, many of those doctrines use verses taken out of context or begin with the false presupposition that Paul started a new religion.

Personally, my greatest anxiety as I undertook this journey was wrestling with the Pauline thought patterns that I had been inculcated with and trying to understand how they had to line up with the rest of Scripture. I knew that Paul said,

> **2 Timothy 3:16-17**
> **All Scripture** is inspired by God and profitable for teaching, for reproof, for correction, for training in righteousness; so that the man of God may be adequate, equipped for every good work.

What I had never considered is that The New Testament wasn't regarded as Scripture when Paul wrote that. In fact, many parts of the New Testament were not even written yet! To Paul, Scripture was the Law and the Prophets, the 'Old' Testament! Let that sink in for a minute!

Further, as I studied, I found that even the Apostles found Paul to be very challenging to understand. He was, after all, one of the greatest Torah scholars of his day - a student of the highly regarded Jewish teacher, Gamaliel (Acts 22:3). That is why Peter said,

2 Peter 3:14-18
Therefore, beloved, since you look for these things, be diligent to be found by Him in peace, spotless and blameless, and regard the patience of our Lord as salvation; just as also **our beloved brother Paul**, according to the wisdom given him, wrote to you, as also in all his letters, speaking in them of these things, **in which are some things hard to understand, which the untaught and unstable distort**, as they do also the rest of the Scriptures, to their own destruction. You therefore, beloved, knowing this beforehand, be on your guard so that you are not carried away by the error of unprincipled men and fall from your own steadfastness, but grow in the grace and knowledge of our Lord and Savior Jesus Christ. This Him be the glory, both now and to the day of eternity. Amen.

Simply, Paul has to line up with the overwhelming evidence of Scripture we have already seen. God is unchanging and His everlasting Torah will be written on our hearts and enforced by the Messiah in the Millennial Kingdom! Paul was steeped in Torah and approached the Good News of the restoration of All Israel from a decidedly Hebraic (Eastern) thought process which is foreign to the Greek (Western) thinker.

Following are several posts exploring Paul and what Scripture actually says. These will challenge our accepted paradigms and begin to lead us to greater truth and a closer adherence to the belief system of the Apostles and the believers in Acts.

The Apostle Paul was NOT a Christian!

Originally Posted on December 2, 2013

Paul never converted to anything.

Christian tradition teaches that Saul, a rabbi, converted to Christianity. In fact, that is a misconception that has developed into a support for mistaken theology and doctrine.

Here is how the story begins according to my New American Standard Bible:

> **Acts 9:1-3**
> The Conversion of Saul
> Now Saul, still breathing threats and murder against the disciples of the Lord, went to the high priest, and asked for letters from him to the synagogues at Damascus, so that if he found any belonging to the Way, both men and women, he might bring them bound to Jerusalem. As he was traveling, it happened that he was approaching Damascus, and suddenly a light from heaven flashed around him . . . .

First, that big paragraph header, 'The Conversion of Saul,' is inserted by the editors. It is not inspired Scripture, and the only thing it does is set the reader up with a false premise!

Read the rest of the chapter and you will see that Saul had an amazing encounter with the risen Messiah. You will see he begins to preach Messiah, but he was not, nor did he ever 'convert' to some other religion!

Here are his own words, some 15 or 20 years later,

> **Acts 23:6**
> Brethren, **I am a Pharisee**, a son of Pharisees; I am on trial for the hope and resurrection of the dead!

He says, '**I AM**,' not, 'I was.'

On two other occasions after his supposed conversion, Paul is quoted as saying, '**I am** a Jew' (Acts 21:39, 22:3).

Not, "I was a Jew..."

Sometime after both of those quotes he says,

Acts 24: 14
But this I admit to you, that according to the Way **which they call a sect** I do serve the God of our fathers, believing <u>everything</u> that is in accordance with the Law and that is written in the Prophets. . . ."

You might ask, 'who are "they?"', and 'a sect of what?'

Well, 'they' are his Jewish accusers, and 'they,' believe him to be a member of a 'sect' of normative first century Judaism named 'the Way.' Notice, his Jewish accusers do not accuse him of being the leader of some other religion.

There are more supporting quotes and statements throughout the Apostolic writings, but why is this important?

This is important because it affects every aspect of our understanding of Paul's writings.

If he was a Jew who never stopped being a Jew; if he was a Pharisee who never stopped being a Pharisee; if he kept Torah and never stopped keeping Torah; then it affects everything we understand about him and about his writings!

Think about it.

Most all theology in the last 1700 years is predicated on the false idea that Saul/Paul rejected the Torah and started a new religion.

His own testimony is that he 'believ[ed] everything in accordance with Law (Torah) and that is written in the Prophets.'

In Deuteronomy 13, the Torah says that anyone, even a prophet with signs and wonders, who teaches any doctrine that leads people away from the commandments of God is to be put to death.

Paul says,

Acts 25:8-11
I have committed no offense either against the Law of the Jews or against the temple or against Caesar. . . . **If, then, I am a wrongdoer and have committed anything worthy of death, I do not refuse to die**; but if none of those things is true of which these men accuse me, no one can hand me over to them. I appeal to Caesar.

He also says,

Acts 28:17-18
Brethren, **though I had done nothing against our people or the customs of our fathers**, yet I was delivered as a prisoner from Jerusalem into the hands of the Romans. And when they had examined me, they were willing to release me because **there was no ground for putting me to death**.

It is a simple and concise case. There are only two possible conclusions:

1. Either Paul indeed was converted to some new Torah-less religion, and then to save his skin he was willing to lie multiple times in a court of law as well as to any who would listen – making him no Apostle at all!

2. Or, **Paul never 'converted' to anything**, but kept Torah and preached the fulfillment of the Jewish hope for the coming of the Holy One of Israel! And, he was willing to suffer and die to get the message to the nations that they could 'come home' and be grafted into Israel!!

Take off the man-made doctrinal filters and read the whole Word.

The Paul who allegedly 'did away with the Law,' wrote,

Romans 3:31

Do we then nullify the law through faith? Absolutely not! Instead **we uphold the law.**

And,

1 Corinthians 7:19
Circumcision is nothing, and uncircumcision is nothing, but **what matters is the keeping of the commandments of God.**

No, Saul/Paul never converted to anything. **He was a Torah-keeping Jew who preached the Gospel of the Kingdom as we can now be grafted into Israel!!**

What was the Apostle Paul's example?

Originally posted on April 21, 2013.

Rav Shaul, the Apostle Paul, made a pretty audacious statement in his first letter to the Corinthians he says,

1 Corinthians 11:1-2
Be imitators of me, just as I also am of Christ. Now I praise you because you remember me in everything and **hold firmly to the traditions, just as I delivered them to you.**

We are to imitate him just as he imitates Yeshua! So, what exactly was Apostle Paul's example? And, what were the 'traditions?'

Good questions! Let's just look at a few verses in the Book of Acts.

Did Rav Shaul keep the feasts?

Acts 20:6, 16
We sailed from Philippi **after the days of Unleavened Bread,** and came to them at Troas within five days; and there we stayed seven days. . . . For Paul had decided to sail past Ephesus so that he would not have to spend time in Asia; for **he was hurrying to be in Jerusalem, if possible, on the day of Pentecost.**

1 Corinthians 5:8
[Speaking of Passover] Therefore **let us celebrate the feast,** not with old leaven, nor with the leaven of malice and wickedness, but with the unleavened bread of sincerity and truth.

What day did Rav Shaul worship on?

Acts 13: 14b
. . . and on **the Sabbath day** they went into the synagogue and sat down.

Acts 13:42-44

As Paul and Barnabas were going out, the people kept begging that these things might be spoken to them **the next Sabbath**. Now when the meeting of the synagogue had broken up, many of the Jews and of the God-fearing proselytes followed Paul and Barnabas, who, speaking to them, were urging them to continue in the grace of God. **The next Sabbath** nearly the whole city assembled to hear the word of the Lord.

Acts 16:13

And on **the Sabbath day** we went outside the gate to a riverside, where we were supposing that there would be a place of prayer; and we sat down and began speaking to the women who had assembled.

There are a dozen more similar references in the book of Acts.

Did Rav Shaul (Apostle Paul) offer sacrifices? (We must be careful to note that Yeshua is the perfect atoning sacrifice, but other sacrifices were not done away with and, at the time of Rav Shaul, could still be lawfully offered in Jerusalem, at the Temple, by Levitical Priests. Scriptural support includes Hebrews 8:4 as well as Ezekiel 43-44, etc.)

Acts 21:26

Then Paul took the men, and the next day, purifying himself along with them, went into the temple giving notice of the completion of the days of purification, until **the sacrifice was offered for each one of them**.

Acts 24:17

Now after several years I came to bring alms to my nation and **to present offerings**;

Did Rav Shaul keep the Torah?

Here is what James explained to Paul about what actions to take to prove that he (Paul) walked in Torah:

Acts 21:24b

. . .and all will know that there is nothing to the things which they have been told about you, but that **you yourself also walk orderly, keeping the Law.**

Acts 21:14b
I do serve the God of our fathers, **believing everything that is in accordance with the Law and that is written in the Prophets.** . . .

Paul said in his own defense,

Acts 25:8
I have committed no offense either against the Law of the Jews or against the temple or against Caesar.

Acts 25:11
If, then, I am a wrongdoer and have committed anything worthy of death [e.g., breaking Torah], I do not refuse to die; but if none of those things is true of which these men accuse me, no one can hand me over to them. I appeal to Caesar.

So, how DID Rav Shaul view himself?

Acts 24:14
But this I admit to you, that **according to the Way which they call a sect** I do serve the God of our fathers, believing everything that is in accordance with the Law and that is written in the Prophets. . . .

Even Rav Shaul's accusers viewed him as leading a sect of Judaism. **NOBODY** thought he was starting some new religion. He was a Torah observant follower of Yeshua haMashiach (Jesus Christ)!

What was James' expectation of Gentiles who came into the faith?

Acts 15:21
For **Moses** from ancient generations has in every city those who preach him, since he is read in the **synagogues** every **Sabbath.**

Rav Shaul, like James, expected new believers to:
- learn Torah (Moses)
- in the synagogue
- on the Sabbath.

Much more could be said about Paul, but that would make this an incredibly long book simply because there are so many paradigms to unlearn. (I contend Paul will be the guy in the New Heaven and Earth who is wearing the neon lime green t-shirt that says, 'I did not say what you think I said!!')

For further in depth study of Paul, I recommend the Pauline Paradox Series by 119 Ministries (see www.119ministries.com). Another good source is J. K. McKee's very scholarly *The New Testament Validates Torah*.

9 REPAIRING THE BREACH

At the very beginning of this challenging book, I shared my desire to be a repairer of the breach and a restorer of the streets on which to dwell. It is a desire I hope you are beginning to experience.

Some may wonder, what is the breach, and why does it need repairing? The answer is involved and long with multiple layers, but the short of it is that by casting aside all things that appeared "Jewish," things like the feasts, Sabbath, and dietary instructions, Christendom perpetuated a divide in our Messiah's Kingdom. The divide actually began much earlier.

Here are two closing posts that provide a general overview, after which I will offer some concluding thoughts on repairing this breach.

The Dividing of Israel and Judah, Then and Now

Originally posted on January 12, 2014.

As I researched and read Scripture related to 'stiffneckedness' for a post, there were multiple connected trails that I chased. Very interesting stuff. . . .

I am not sure quite how I got into the passage leading to this post, however, the connection to 'stiff necks' is readily apparent.

On various occasions I have discussed the division of Israel and Judah, how they are often named 'the House of Israel,' and the 'House of Judah' in Scripture, and how this has particular prophetic significance. A GREAT primer, if the subject is new to you, is *The Lost Sheep* by 119 Ministries.com. (They have MANY terrific teaching – all free!)

Now, we understand that the division was in the plan of Yahweh (1 Kings 12:24), though I think only in recent years have we begun to understand the hows and whys. Today, as Yahweh reveals an understanding of things long hidden in Scripture, we find Him preparing Israel to be rejoined to Judah . . . to the consternation of many.

What I want to share is what I read and pondered the other day.

Jeroboam, the first king of Israel (the Northern Ten Tribes), was **very intentional** in separating **to himself** the Northern Kingdom. He had a kingdom and he wanted to ensure that He and his progeny kept it! I mean, who wants to go back to normal life when you can build a dynasty?

Let's read and then discuss and compare:

I Kings 12:25-33
Then Jeroboam built Shechem in the hill country of Ephraim, and lived there. And he went out from there and built Penuel. Jeroboam said in his heart, **"Now the kingdom will return to the house of David. If this**

people go up to offer sacrifices in the house of the Lord at Jerusalem, then the heart of this people will return to their lord, even to Rehoboam king of Judah; and they will kill me and return to Rehoboam king of Judah." So the king consulted, and made two golden calves, and he said to them, "**It is too much for you to go up to Jerusalem; behold your gods, O Israel,** that brought you up from the land of Egypt." He set one in Bethel, and the other he put in Dan. Now **this thing became a sin, for the people went to worship before the one as far as Dan.** And he **made houses on high places,** and **made priests from among all the people who were not of the sons of Levi.** Jeroboam **instituted a feast in the eighth month on the fifteenth day of the month, like the feast which is in Judah,** and he went up to the altar; thus he did in Bethel, sacrificing to the calves which he had made. And **he stationed in Bethel the priests of the high places which he had made.** Then he went up to the altar which he had made in Bethel on the fifteenth day in the eighth month, even **in the month which he had devised in his own heart; and he instituted a feast for the sons of Israel and went up to the altar to burn incense.**

WOW!! That passage just boggles the mind! And, it begins a pattern of behavior that continues to this very day.

Scripture is clear. The reason Jeroboam did what he did was to drive a wedge between Israel and Judah, to create division between the people and Jerusalem, the dwelling place of Yahweh. He did so with several very specific measures. He –

- redefined their God.
- redefined their worship.
- established a system of priests.
- instituted new holy days (holidays).
- syncretized paganism into the religious system.

This is a calculated transgression against Yahweh, and against His Torah. The gravity is breath-taking in its coldness! This is a major milestone in the House of Israel's rejection of Yahweh and HIS ways, His voice, His commandments, His Torah, etc.

That rejection continues to this very day!

Predictably, so does the sin of Jeroboam.

An honest ramble through church history, particularly if you look through the unapproved, unsanitized history, reveals that at numerous points in history, especially in the late 2nd to 5th centuries, Christendom's Greco-Roman Bishops were very intentional in dividing the restored Tent of David that the Apostles began rebuilding. (The Amos 9:11ff quote, cited by James in Acts 15:15ff has an early partial fulfillment, but we see that it is pointed to the end of days.)

To take a very quick overview of Christendom, let's consider a few things the church fathers did. They,

- redefined God. Torah-keeping Yeshua became Torah-abolishing Jesus. (Some attempt to tap dance around this charge by stating that the 'principles' still apply, but Torah is done away and 'we don't have to do that.')
- redefined worship by removing a number of things tied directly to the Hebrew roots of the Messiah and the faith.
- established a system of priests that operated according to their own doctrines and thought processes. All Hebraic perspectives and contextual clues were removed, ignored or denigrated.
- instituted new holy days (holidays), such as Christmas, Lent, Easter, etc., and erased, denigrated, and ignored the Feasts of Yahweh that were tied to the Creation Order and the sanctifying will of the Father.
- syncretized paganism into their new religious system with a myriad of false practices.

No doubt, some pastor reading this is now holding his head in his hands and thinks I have completely lost my mind. Rest assured, I have done the research and I make NO excuses for the errors I walked in while occupying a pulpit for a decade.

Yes, there are true believers saved in the name of Jesus, but there is also truth coming out all over and we have a choice to make. Learn, repent and humbly correct our errors in order to prepare for THE Kingdom, or move forward with stiff necks and hard hearts protecting our reputation and little kingdoms. Once we have been informed, we have to do something about it, or we walk in willful sin.

Jeroboam chose the latter and Scripture records that Abba Yahweh warned him. This is what happened,

1 Kings 13:33-34
After this event Jeroboam did not return from his evil way, but again he made priests of the high places from among all the people; any who would, he ordained, to be priests of the high places. This event became sin to the house of Jeroboam, even to blot it out and destroy it from off the face of the earth.

In the last decade, at an accelerating pace, the Holy Spirit has been awakening people to the ancient paths (Jeremiah 6:16-19). We are being awakened to the huge amount of tradition and pagan myth we have allowed into our worship, and we are, most importantly, awakening to the historical fact of the intentional dividing of Judah and Gentile believers in Messiah. In the wake of this growing tidal wave of search for truth and a restoration of first century practice, there is also a growing number of pastors who, when faced with this information, choose to continue in the path of Jeroboam.

Truly sad, but even sadder are the words of Messiah Yeshua,

Matthew 7:21-23
Not everyone who says to Me, 'Lord, Lord,' will enter the kingdom of heaven, but **he who does the will of My**

Father who is in heaven will enter. Many will say to Me on that day, 'Lord, Lord, did we not prophesy in Your name, and in Your name cast out demons, and in Your name perform many miracles?' And then I will declare to them, 'I never knew you; **depart from Me, you who practice <u>lawlessness.</u>'**

Notice the distinction between 'the will of My Father' and 'lawlessness.' Even a simple reading of the Tanak, the 'Old Testament', indicates that 'the will of My Father' is to 'obey My voice,' 'walk in My paths,' 'keep My commandments,' etc., and of course, 'lawlessness' is walking counter to/rejecting the Torah.

We are at a pivotal point in history as we enter the seventh millennium. Our Father is at the point of bringing His people together to again walk in His ways and follow the Messiah as we enter through His redemptive blood. We dare not stand in His way by dividing Israel and Judah. Rather, we best be seeking Him in humility and asking how we can be of service!

I know this is challenging for some. A heart of humility and prayer is the answer.

The Sin of Israel and Modern Christendom

Originally posted on January 13, 2014.

In the previous post, we looked at Jeroboam and his intentional dividing of Israel from Judah. He did so by developing and encouraging false worship.

In this post, we want to read a passage from 2 Kings 17 that may sound uncomfortably like reading a modern Christian magazine. I'll put a visual of the passage below and only quote select verses. I encourage you to read the whole passage and ponder the gravity and sheer rebellion, both then, and now.

First, let's read a couple verses from the middle of the passage to remind us of the points from the previous post. Jeroboam was intentional in dividing Israel from Judah.

2 Kings 17:21-23
When He had torn Israel from the house of David, they made Jeroboam the son of Nebat king. Then **Jeroboam drove Israel away from following the Lord** and made them commit a great sin. **The sons of Israel walked in all the sins of Jeroboam** which he did; they did not depart from them until the Lord removed Israel from His sight, as He spoke through all His servants the prophets. So **Israel was carried away into exile** from their own land to Assyria **until this day.**

Israel was not innocent. They followed and their hearts were exposed! But, Jeroboam led. He had counselors around him and religious leaders who aided, but he shouldered the initial responsibility.

Earlier in the passage we read,

2 Kings 17:13-15
. . . **the Lord warned Israel** and Judah through all His prophets and every seer, saying, **"Turn from your evil ways and keep My commandments, My statutes**

according to all the TORAH which I commanded your fathers, and which I sent to you through My servants the prophets." However, **they did not listen,** but stiffened their neck like their fathers, who did not believe in the Lord their God. **They rejected His statutes and His covenant** which He made with their fathers and His warnings with which He warned them. And they followed vanity and became vain, and went after the nations which surrounded them, concerning which the Lord had commanded them not to do like them.

Israel was warned!! (I am not avoiding Judah, but Ezekiel 23 and several other passages clearly demonstrate that Jeroboam led Israel and Israel led Judah.) The prophets cried out to Israel begging her to teshuv, to return, repent. She would have none of it. Her neck stiffened at the warnings and she, in her own will, pursued false worship and the ways of the pagan nations that surrounded her.

2 Kings 17:7-8
Now this came about because the sons of Israel had sinned against the Lord their God, who had brought them up from the land of Egypt from under the hand of Pharaoh, king of Egypt, and they had feared other gods **and walked in the customs of the nations whom the Lord had driven out** before the sons of Israel, and in the customs of the kings of Israel which they had introduced. . . .

What customs of the pagans? Many, actually. Here are a few.
- Astarte/Asherah, the pagan fertility goddess often worshiped in the spring with rituals that included eggs dyed in the blood of sacrificed babies, was one of the abominations that Israel picked us from the nations. Astarte is also called Ishtar. Get it?
- Molech was an idol that the ancient pagans sacrificed children to. They would heat a bronze or cast iron image of the deity until it was cherry red, then place

169

their child into the lap or bosom of the abomination. Cherry red (suits) with children in the laps. Hmmm. . . . We see something like that around the Winter solstice every year.

- They set up Asherah poles. Tall pointing obelisks with overt phallic symbolism that looked like the one that actually came from Egypt that sits in the middle of Vatican Square. Do a search for pictures of the monstrosity. Notice the sun disk underneath? Or, is that to represent something else?

The connections to modern church buildings and practice are stunning.

'But Pete, we don't do THAT! We worship the God of heaven and earth! And, those holy days and emblems aren't really connected with those gods. I mean, that's not what it means to ME!'

What it means to you or me or anyone else does not matter compared to what it means to Yahweh. What does Yahweh see when He sees this pagan syncretism in churches? He heard the screams of every one of those children. **Do you think He forgot?**

More from 2 Kings 17,

> ### 2 Kings 17:32-33
> **They also feared the Lord** and appointed from among themselves priests of the high places, who acted for them in the houses of the high places. **They feared the Lord and served their own gods according to the custom of the nations** from among whom they had been carried away into exile.

Brothers and sisters, they THOUGHT they were doing something that was okay. They even FEARED YAHWEH!! But **they were stiff necked and disobedient!** He said, 'DO NOT worship Me the way the pagans do!'

> ### 2 Kings 17:34-36

To this day they do according to the earlier customs: they do not fear the Lord, <u>nor do they follow their statutes or their ordinances or the TORAH, or the commandments which the Lord commanded the sons of Jacob</u>, whom He named Israel; with whom the Lord made a covenant and commanded them, saying, "You shall not fear other gods, nor bow down yourselves to them nor serve them nor sacrifice to them. But the Lord, who brought you up from the land of Egypt with great power and with an outstretched arm, Him you shall fear, and to Him you shall bow yourselves down, and to Him you shall sacrifice.

Yep, '**to this day**', the church does as the pagans do. The church follows the Roman Catholic adoption of many pagan traditions and customs. Look it up! Do the research. Start with an encyclopedia, public library or Google. Turning a blind eye is rule #1 in *Stiff Necked for Dummies*.

Catholicism loved the sun god and incorporated many things from Mithras worship and Asherah/Baal worship . . . from SUNday to red pointy hats and halos. Look it up!

What is it that Yahweh said?

<u>2 Kings 17:37-39</u>
The statutes and the ordinances and the law and the commandment which He wrote for you, **you shall observe to do <u>forever;</u>** and you shall not fear other gods. The covenant that I have made with you, you shall not forget, nor shall you fear other gods. But the Lord your God you shall fear; and He will deliver you from the hand of all your enemies."

Sadly, the passage ends,

<u>2 Kings 17:40-41</u>
However, **they did not listen, but they did according to their earlier custom**. So while <u>these nations feared the Lord, they also served their idols</u>; their children likewise

and their grandchildren, as their fathers did, so they do to this day.

Believers in the God of the Bible have GOT to wake up and face the music. Repent from the pagan syncretism we have inherited! Return to the ancient paths that God said are 'forever.'

We are exactly paralleling ancient Israel. We do what is right in our own eyes and call it good.

Modern Christendom IS committing the sin of Israel. There is a remedy!

Revelation 18:4-8
I heard another voice from heaven, saying, "**Come out of her, my people, so that you will not participate in her sins and receive of her plagues**; for her sins have piled up as high as heaven, and God has remembered her iniquities. Pay her back even as she has paid, and give back to her double according to her deeds; in the cup which she has mixed, mix twice as much for her. To the degree that she glorified herself and lived sensuously, to the same degree give her torment and mourning; for she says in her heart, 'I sit as a queen and I am not a widow, and will never see mourning.' For this reason in one day her plagues will come, pestilence and mourning and famine, and she will be burned up with fire; for the Lord God who judges her is strong.

GET. OUT. OF. BABYLON!!

As we saw in the Amos 9 passage at the beginning of the book, repairing the breach and restoring the streets on which to dwell are part of the restoration of the fallen tent of David that happens 'in that day.' I believe we are 'in that day.' The Tent of David is being restored and prepared for the Lion of the Tribe of Judah.

Isaiah gives a specific and measured step toward repairing with particular blessings attached. Notice the 'if-then' statement.

Isaiah 58:12-14

Those from among you will rebuild the ancient ruins; you will raise up the age-old foundations; and you will be called the repairer of the breach, the restorer of the streets in which to dwell. **If because of the Sabbath**, you turn your foot from doing your own pleasure on My holy day, and **call the Sabbath a delight**, the holy day of the Lord honorable, and honor it, desisting from your own ways, from seeking your own pleasure and speaking your own word, **then you will take delight in the Lord, and I will make you ride on the heights of the earth; and I will feed you with the heritage of Jacob your father**, for the mouth of the Lord has spoken.

Repairing the breach begins with individual, or personal, repentance and obedience. We must each acknowledge our sin in walking contrary to YHVH's everlasting covenant. While Christendom most certainly has many things right, it is those lawless things that are contrary to His covenant that we must repent of.

Repentance, teshuva, is turning TO the ancient paths. Our Messiah, by His atoning blood, has allowed us to be grafted into Israel, we now must learn to 'walk as He walked.'

As we repent individually, we must then repent corporately. We must confess that we have walked contrary to His ways and His instructions in righteousness. We must repent of the doctrines that led to division and caused the breach between Judah and the early followers of Messiah who turned away from the Torah. Only then can we become truly useful in the restoration of the Kingdom and the whole House of Israel.

Once we have repented, our next step is to share what we are learning, in a loving manner, with those around us as we become ambassadors for our Messiah. (Give away copies of this book, tell the story, pass along websites, etc.) Yeshua, by His own words in Matthew 15:24, came 'for the lost sheep of the house of Israel.' We, as His ambassadors, must do the same as we lead others to repentance. We carry forward the mission of gathering the lost sheep through reconciliation and bridges of trust, peace and righteousness.

I pray you will join me in being a repairer of the breach and a restorer of the streets on which to dwell!

Resources

Following are some resources for further study.

At the time of publishing, I consider all of these resources to be trustworthy. There are many others, but these are some I am most familiar with.

The basics:
- natsab.com
- teshuvaministries.net/getting-started/
- 119ministries.com
- thebarkingfox.com/
- hebroots.com/

For deeper study into covenants, words, Hebrew, etc.:
- wisdomintorah.com/
- wildbranch.org/
- billcloud.org/

Additional links of note:

- http://houseofdavidfellowship.com/whywebelievewhat webelieve.htm

ABOUT THE AUTHOR

Pete Rambo, 49, was raised on the mission field in Colombia, South America by parents who love and serve the Lord. After several mission trips as a teen, Pete graduated from Erskine College and entered the US Army expecting to be a career officer. Yahweh had other plans. In the spring of 1991, after returning from Desert Shield/Storm with the 82nd Airborne Division, he met Kelly, an Army dental hygienist. During the time they were dating, Kelly survived a near fatal parachuting accident that resulted in her being 100% disabled. They married in January 1992 before Pete left for Ranger School.

Needing to stay closer to Kelly and help in her disability, Pete left the military in 1993 and bounced through various businesses and positions while avoiding the call to ministry. Finally, in 1998, at the time of his father's funeral, he submitted to his patient Heavenly Father and went the 'traditional route' to seminary. In 2002 he graduated with a Masters of Divinity from Columbia International University's Seminary and School of Missions and began pastoring a small Associate Reformed Presbyterian Church in central South Carolina. He was there for ten years and then, after a short interim, began helping to lead a Messianic Fellowship in Prosperity, SC.

During most of his life, Pete has had a particular interest in eschatology (end times events/prophecy) and in understanding truth. (He says, tongue in cheek, 'I used to be a conspiracy theorist . . . now, I am a conspiracy factualist.') In his quest, he began to run into pieces of information that challenged his very conservative traditional Christian religious perspectives. Only when he began to pray earnestly for Yahweh to show him TRUTH did Yahweh move his focus from geopolitical events onto a close scrutiny of the practices of the Church. As he learned how far the Church had moved from the simplicity of the Book of Acts and the clear teaching of the Word, he became convicted of the need for a personal reformation.

He is still learning how to truly follow Paul (1 Cor. 11:1-2) in the Way (Acts24:14), but he believes much headway has been made through coming out of Babylon (Rev. 18:4) and embracing the Hebrew roots of Yeshua (Jesus) his Messiah and walking as Yeshua walked. The blessings he and his family have enjoyed as a result of obedience to the whole Word of God are innumerable.

In 2013, he began a blog, natsab.com, for the purpose of sharing his journey as well as explaining what he was learning. His greatest joy is sharing the roots of the faith and seeing another person return to the ancient paths that our Messiah walked.

Pete and Kelly have a family of four boys. They homeschool and raise the boys on a micro farm where, in addition to following Messiah, they learn and practice skills in self-sufficiency as it relates to food. They have dairy goats, honey bees, raised beds, laying hens, fruit trees, etc.

Peter G. Rambo, Sr.

Scripture Index

Gen. 1:14 (143)
Gen. 1:31-2:2 (59)
Gen. 2:2-3 (61, 73)
Gen. 3:8 (102)
Gen. 9:12-17 (66)
Gen. 9:8-17 (41)
Gen 15:1 (105)
Gen 15:6 (102)
Gen 16:7-13 (113)
Gen 16:8-15 (109)
Gen 17:1-11 (42)
Gen. 17:7-8 (11)
Gen. 22:11-18 (113)
Gen. 26:4-5 (92)
Exo. 3:1-5 (108)
Exo. 3:2-6 (113)
Exo. 3:15 (6)
Exo. 12:14, 24 (133)
Exo. 12:38(17)
Exo. 12:49(16)
Exo. 14:19 (114)
Exo. 14:24 (114)
Exo. 16:22-30 (73)
Exo. 16:25-30 (57)
Exo. 18:20 (52)
Exo. 19:16-17 (104)
Exo. 20:8-11 (74)
Exo. 20:9-11 (57)
Exo. 23:12 (57)
Exo. 24:9-11 (103)
Exo. 24:9-11 (115)
Exo. 31:12-17 (25, 44, 57, 66, 96)
Exo. 31:14-17 (74)

Exo. 31:16-17 (12)
Exo. 34 (125)
Exo. 34:21 (58)
Exo. 35:2 (58)
Lev. 11:44-45 (94)
Lev. 19 (133)
Lev. 23 (20, 71, 95, 143)
Lev. 23:1-4 (75)
Lev. 23:2-4 (58)
Lev. 23:14,21,31,41 (12)
Num. 15:14-16 (16)
Num. 15:15-16 (12)
Num. 15:32-36 (62)
Num. 21:9 (38)
Num. 22:22-35 (114)
Duet. 5:12-15 (58, 75)
Duet. 5:29 (93)
Duet. 6:24-25 (48)
Duet. 6:25 (93)
Deut. 12:29-32 (24, 40)
Duet. 12:32-13:5 (97)
Duet. 12:32-13:11 (87)
Duet. 13:1-5 (126)
Duet. 18:18 (126)
Duet. 23:14 (115)
Joshua 22:5 (52)
Judges 2:1-4 (114)
Judges 2:1-5 (111)
Judges 6:11-23 (114)
Judges 13 (110)
Judges 13:17-18 (110)
Judges 13:2-23 (114)
Ruth 1:16-17 (16)
2 Sam. 7:13-16 (11)

2 Sam. 22:21-25 (47)
1 Kings 12:24-33 (158)
1 Kings 12:25-33 (38)
1 Kings 13:33-34 (161)
2 Kings 17: 7-8 (164)
2 Kings 17:13-15 (163)
2 Kings 17:21-23 (163)
2 Kings 17:32-36 (165)
2 Kings 17: 37-41 (166)
2 Kings 18:1 (38)
2 Chron. 7:14-16 (11)
Job 23:10-11 (46)
Psalm 2:7-12 (134)
Psalm 19:7 (52)
Psalm 19:7-14 (53)
Psalm 40:8 (53)
Psalm 97: 7-13 (98)
Psalm 105:8,10 (11)
Psalm 119 (99)
Psalm 119:1 (52)
Psalm 119:4 (52)
Psalm 119:44-45 (12)
Psalm 119: 111-112 (12)
Psalm 119:165 (52)
Psalm 136 (11)
Prov. 3:1-2 (52)
Prov. 4:2 (126)
Prov. 6:23 (52
Isa. 2:1-5 (127, 140)
Isa. 2:3-4 (134)
Isa. 2:3-5 (52)
Isa. 8:20 (52)
Isa. 9:6 (111)
Isa. 40:8 (91)
Isa. 42:8 (8)
Isa. 42:21 (140)
Isa. 42:21-22 (122)
Isa. 52:4 (52)
Isa. 56:6-7 (64)
Isa. 58:12 (2)
Isa. 58: 12-14 (167)

Isa. 65:1-7 (13)
Isa. 66:16-17 (13, 95)
Isa. 66:16-24 (59, 122)
Isa. 66: 22-23 (133)
Isa. 66:22-23 (64, 76)
Isa. 66:23(13)
Jer. 6:16-19 (46, 50, 161)
Jer. 11:16 (15)
Jer. 16:19 (44)
Jer. 16:19-21 (30)
Jer. 16:21 (7)
Jer. 31:31-34 (127)
Jer. 31:31-37 (44)
Jer. 31:33 (119)
Jer. 31:35-37 (67)
Jer. 32:35-37 (134)
Jer. 33:14-22 (128)
Jer. 44:23 (53)
Ezek. 37:11-19 (17)
Ezek. 37:24-28 (11, 43, 94)
Ezek. 43-44 (86, 133)
Dan. 9:11 (53)
Hos. 12:5 (8)
Joel 2:32 (8)
Amos 3:7 (73, 127)
Amos 5:8 (8)
Amos 9:9-15 (2)
Amos 9:11 (160)
Micah 4:2-3 (134)
Zech. 13:9 (8)
Zech. 14:16-19 (13,25)
Zech. 14:16-21 (122, 133)
Zech. 14:21 (86)
Mal. 2:6-8 (52)
Mal. 3:6 (63, 73)
Mal. 4:1-6 (30, 145)
Mal. 4: 4-6 (133)
Matt. 5:17-19 (25, 76, 126)
Matt. 5:17-20 (118)
Matt. 5:18 (67)
Matt. 5:19 (83)

Matt. 7:21-23 (161)
Matt. 7:28 (126)
Matt. 22:36-40 (119)
Matt. 23:39 (8)
Mark 16:2 (71)
Mark 16:9-20 (71)
Luke 5:12, 17 (71)
Luke 8:22 (71)
Luke 15:9-10 (32)
Luke 24:13-35 (141)
Luke 24:27 (113)
John 1:1-3 (102)
John 1:18 (104, 109, 113)
John 5:37 (113)
John 5:45-47 (113)
John 6:46 (104, 106)
John 7:16 (90, 121, 126)
John 14:15 (105, 121)
Acts 1:5-7 (143)
Acts 1:6-7 (141)
Acts 2:11 (69)
Acts 2:42, 46 (69)
Acts 3:31 (87)
Acts 6:13-14 (84)
Acts 7:37-38 (106)
Acts 9:1-3 (149)
Acts 10 (95)
Acts 10:28 (95)
Acts 13:14 (153)
Acts 13:42-44 (68, 77, 154)
Acts 15 (142)
Acts 15:15 (160)
Acts 15:20-21 (21)
Acts 15:21 (155)
Acts 16:13 (154)
Acts 20:18 (69)
Acts 20:6,16 (21, 153)
Acts 20:7 (66-72)
Acts 20:9 (69)
Acts 21:14 (155)
Acts 21:20 (85)

Acts 21:21-26 (21)
Acts 21:24 (154)
Acts 21:26 (85, 154)
Acts 21: 39 (150)
Acts 22:3 (148, 150)
Acts 23:6 (149)
Acts 24:13-15 (21)
Acts 24:14 (150, 155)
Acts 24:17 (154)
Acts 25:7-11 (21)
Acts 25:7-8 (86)
Acts 25:8 (155)
Acts 25:8-11 (151)
Acts 25:11 (155)
Acts 28: 17-18 (21, 151)
Rom. 3:31 (151)
Rom. 7:7 (53)
Rom. 9-11 (144)
Rom. 9:6-8 (17)
Rom. 9:25-26 (144)
Rom. 11:17-24 (14)
Rom. 11:21-22 (15)
Rom. 11:33-36 (105)
1 Cor. 5:8 (21, 153)
1 Cor. 7:19 (152)
1 Cor. 11:1-2 (153)
1 Cor. 16:2 (68,69)
2 Cor. 6:14-7:1 (49)
Eph. 2:12 (96, 127)
Col. 1:15 (115)
Col. 1:16-17 (102)
Col. 2:17 (21)
1 Thes. 5:1-4 (143, 144)
2 Tim. 3:16-17 (147)
Heb. 8:8 (122)
Heb. 13:8 (89)
James 1:25 (52)
James 4:12 (105)
2 Pet. 3:14-17 (128)
2 Pet. 3:14-18 (148)
2 Pet. 3:15-17 (88)

1 John 3:4 (53, 89)

Rev. 18: 4-8 (167)

Rev. 20:1-7 (122)

Rev. 22:14 (52)

Peter G. Rambo, Sr.

Made in the USA
San Bernardino, CA
30 December 2016